ASSYRIA

GREECE

MEDIA

MACEDONIA

CHALDEA

CARTHAGE

PERSIA

ROME

The First 3000 Years:
ANCIENT CIVILIZATIONS OF THE TIGRIS, EUPHRATES, AND NILE RIVER VALLEYS, AND THE MEDITERRANEAN SEA

QUEEN SHUB-AD OF UR

This royal lady lived under the hot sun of Sumer more than five thousand years ago! Here, she wears a black wig covered with a decorative headdress made of gold, lapis lazuli, and carnelian. Her fragmentary remains were found surrounded by those of twenty-five court attendants, killed to accompany her to a future life.

The First 3000 Years:

ANCIENT CIVILIZATIONS OF THE TIGRIS, EUPHRATES, AND NILE RIVER VALLEYS, AND THE MEDITERRANEAN SEA

WRITTEN & ILLUSTRATED BY

C. B. Falls

New York

PUBLISHED BY THE VIKING PRESS

To Bedelia

Contents

List of Illustrations

CRO-MAGNONS

These primitive artists are Cro-Magnons—a people who lived in northern Spain and southern France and who are believed to be the direct ancestors of modern man. Here in a Spanish cave at Altamira are found amazing and facile drawings of the various animals they hunted—bison, reindeer, and horses—drawn with such skill that civilized man has never surpassed them.

The Theme of this Book

"Civilization," according to the dictionary, "is an advanced state of human society in which a high level of art, science, religion, and government has been reached."

11

Man has lived on earth more than a quarter of a million years, but he has been "civilized" for only five or six thousand. During all the long ages before, he was a barbarian, a Stone Age man, with a primitive culture. No one can say that exactly at a certain point he crossed the line between barbarism and civilization; it happened by a slow process of evolution, one that is still going on. But archaeologists have uncovered the approximate beginnings.

Our civilization began in the "fertile crescent" of the Near East between 4000 and 3000 B. C.

Somewhat later, in the Far Eastern half of the world, India and China began developing their wonderful ancient cultures. But this is not their story. This is the story of the oldest cradle of civilization, of the first civilized nations that grew up around the Mediterranean Sea, from which our own Western culture has sprung.

Actually, civilized *ways* in the West started way back in the Stone Age. When Cro-Magnon man drew reindeer, mammoths, bison and boars on the walls of a cave in Altamira, Spain, thirteen thousand years ago, he had added art and religion to an advanced hunting culture. Prehistoric European lake-dwellers had real villages, with wooden houses built on piles in the water, and the rudiments of social living. And when the first farmers learned to plant wild wheat and barley—somewhere in the Eastern Mediterranean area around 8000 B. C.—they had launched the "neolithic revolution" that would turn man into a food-producer.

Why, then, if the origins of Western civilization go far back into the dim ages, does its history begin in the fourth millennium B. C.? Because in that crucial time, in the same region where agriculture started, men began to live in cities and make written records of what they had done. And history is a tale pieced together from writings as well as from archaeological discoveries.

Records in the Western world were first made in settlements along two river valleys in the Near East, the valley of the Nile and the valley of the Tigris and Euphrates Rivers in Mesopotamia. Here the earliest advances of ancient civilization were set down on clay tablets and stone palettes. From those two valleys, civilization spread as people came in contact with one another through trading or wars. It spread up and down the rivers and around the shores of the Mediterranean Sea. Sometimes its progress was stopped, and it seemed as if people were going backward. But then it moved forward again.

After a little more than three thousand years, at the death of Augustus, the Western "civilized world" comprised the vast Roman Empire. The whole Mediterranean area had achieved a "high level of art, science, religion, and government" — and was ready to pass it on to all of Europe.

This book pictures and tells the story of those first three thousand years.

The Maps

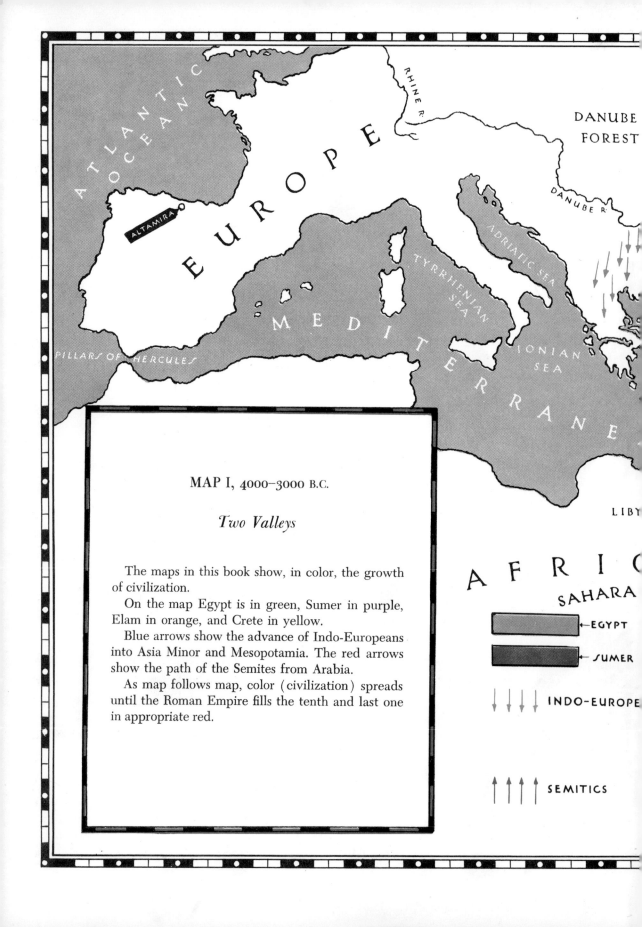

RHINE R.

DANUBE
FOREST

DANUBE R.

ATLANTIC

OCEANIC

EUROPE

ALTAMIRA

ADRIATIC SEA

TYRRHENIAN SEA

IONIAN SEA

PILLARS OF HERCULES

MEDITERRANE

LIBY

AFRIC

SAHARA

MAP I, 4000–3000 B.C.

Two Valleys

The maps in this book show, in color, the growth of civilization.

On the map Egypt is in green, Sumer in purple, Elam in orange, and Crete in yellow.

Blue arrows show the advance of Indo-Europeans into Asia Minor and Mesopotamia. The red arrows show the path of the Semites from Arabia.

As map follows map, color (civilization) spreads until the Roman Empire fills the tenth and last one in appropriate red.

←EGYPT

←SUMER

↓↓↓↓ INDO-EUROPE

↑↑↑↑ SEMITICS

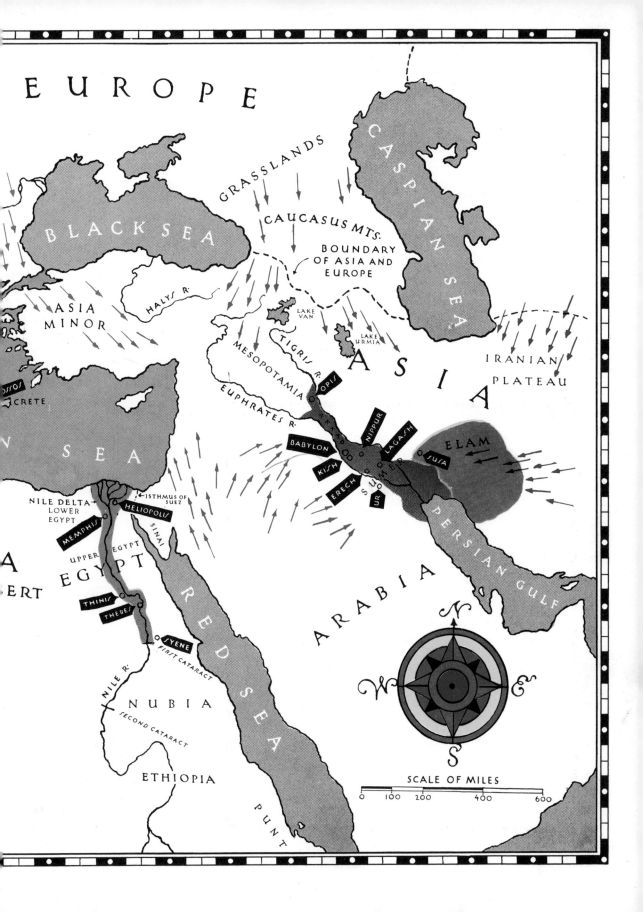

EUROPE

BLACK SEA

GRASSLANDS

CAUCASUS MTS.
BOUNDARY
OF ASIA AND
EUROPE

CASPIAN SEA

ASIA MINOR

HALYS R.

LAKE VAN

LAKE URMIA

ASIA

IRANIAN PLATEAU

MESOPOTAMIA

TIGRIS R.

EUPHRATES R.

OPIS

NIPPUR

LAGASH

ELAM

SUSA

BABYLON

KISH

ERECH

SUMER

UR

SEA

CRETE

NILE DELTA-
LOWER
EGYPT

HELIOPOLIS

ISTHMUS OF SUEZ

MEMPHIS

UPPER EGYPT

SINAI

EGYPT

PERSIAN GULF

DESERT

THINIS

THEBES

RED SEA

ARABIA

SYENE
FIRST CATARACT

NILE R.

NUBIA

SECOND CATARACT

ETHIOPIA

PUNT

N
W   E
S

SCALE OF MILES
0   100   200   400   600

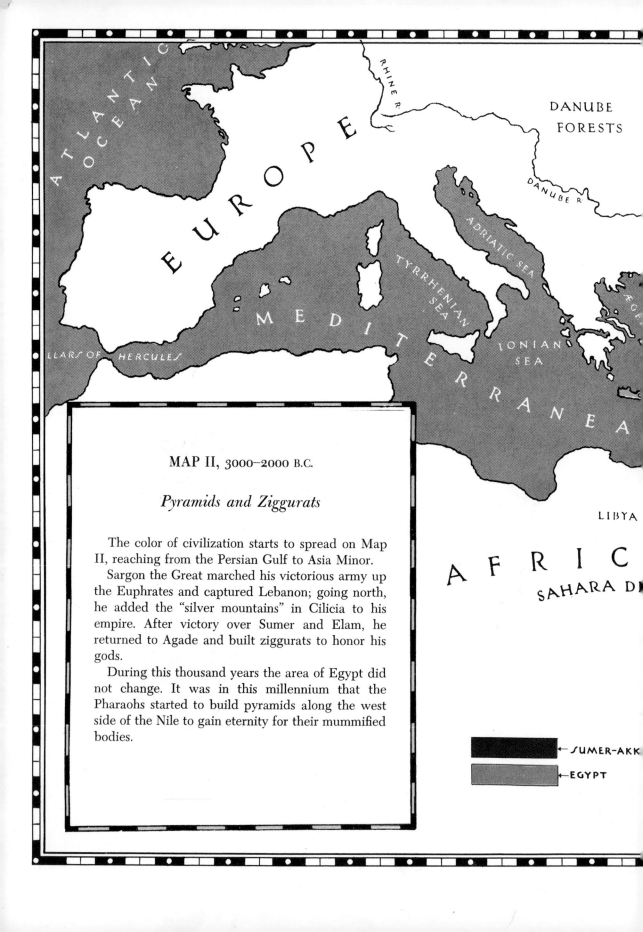

ATLANTIC OCEAN

EUROPE

RHINE R.

DANUBE FORESTS

DANUBE R.

ADRIATIC SEA

TYRRHENIAN SEA

MEDITERRANEAN

IONIAN SEA

PILLARS OF HERCULES

LIBYA

AFRICA

SAHARA D

MAP II, 3000–2000 B.C.

Pyramids and Ziggurats

The color of civilization starts to spread on Map II, reaching from the Persian Gulf to Asia Minor.

Sargon the Great marched his victorious army up the Euphrates and captured Lebanon; going north, he added the "silver mountains" in Cilicia to his empire. After victory over Sumer and Elam, he returned to Agade and built ziggurats to honor his gods.

During this thousand years the area of Egypt did not change. It was in this millennium that the Pharaohs started to build pyramids along the west side of the Nile to gain eternity for their mummified bodies.

←SUMER-AKK

←EGYPT

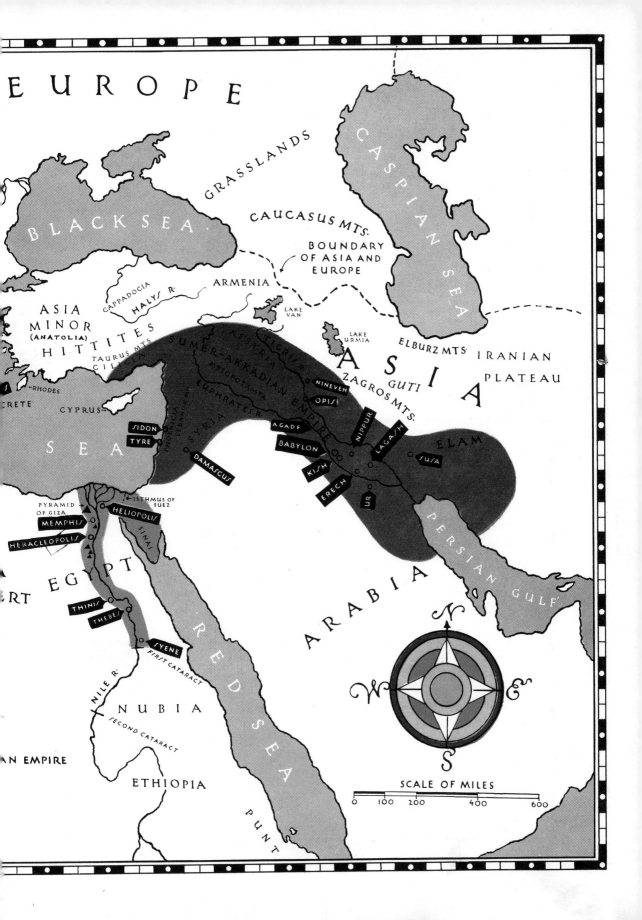

EUROPE

BLACK SEA

GRASSLANDS

CAUCASUS MTS.

CASPIAN SEA

BOUNDARY
OF ASIA AND
EUROPE

ARMENIA

LAKE
VAN

LAKE
URMIA

ELBURZ MTS. IRANIAN

ASIA
MINOR
(ANATOLIA)

CAPPADOCIA

HALYS R.

PLATEAU

HITTITES

TAURUS MTS.
CILICIA

ASSYRIA

TIGRIS R.

A S I A

ZAGROS MTS.

GUTI

RHODES

CRETE

SUMER-AKKADIAN EMPIRE

MESOPOTAMIA

NINEVEH

OPIS

CYPRUS

EUPHRATES R.

PHOENICIA
LEBANON

SIDON

TYRE

SYRIA

AGADE

BABYLON

NIPPUR

LAGASH

SUSA

ELAM

S E A

DAMASCUS

KISH

ERECH

UR

ISTHMUS OF
SUEZ

PYRAMID
OF GIZA

HELIOPOLIS

MEMPHIS

HERACLEOPOLIS

SINAI

P E R S I A N   G U L F

E G Y P T

A R A B I A

RT

THINI

THEBES

SYENE

FIRST CATARACT

R E D   S E A

N

AN EMPIRE

NUBIA

NILE R.

W

E

SECOND CATARACT

ETHIOPIA

S

SCALE OF MILES

P U N T

0   100   200   400   600

ATLANTIC OCEAN

RHINE R.

DANUBE R.

EUROPE

ADRIATIC SEA

TYRRHENIAN SEA

IONIAN SEA

MEDITERRANE

MY TI

CRETE

AFRIC

SAHARA DESE

MAP III, 2000–1580 B.C.

The Scene Widens:
Babylonia, Hatti, Egypt, Crete

Here spread before you are the kingdoms of Babylonia, Hatti, and Egypt.

Babylonia: About 2100 B.C., Semitic Amorites from Syria descended the Euphrates, captured and fortified a small town called Babylon. War broke out at once between the empire of Sumer-Akkad and the invaders. Hammurabi, the greatest king of Babylon, eventually captured Sumer-Akkad, which became part of the Babylonian Empire. Beginning in the eighteenth century B.C., barbarian Kassites invaded Babylonia and ruled it for approximately six hundred years.

Hatti: About 1800 B.C. a tribe of Indo-Europeans called Hittites, from north of the Black Sea, migrated into Asia Minor and founded a confederation of city-states.

Egypt: About 1675 B.C. the barbarian Hyksos invaded the Delta and built a fortified city called Avaris. They ruled Egypt for nearly a century before they were driven out.

←EGYPT

←BABYLONIA

←HATTI

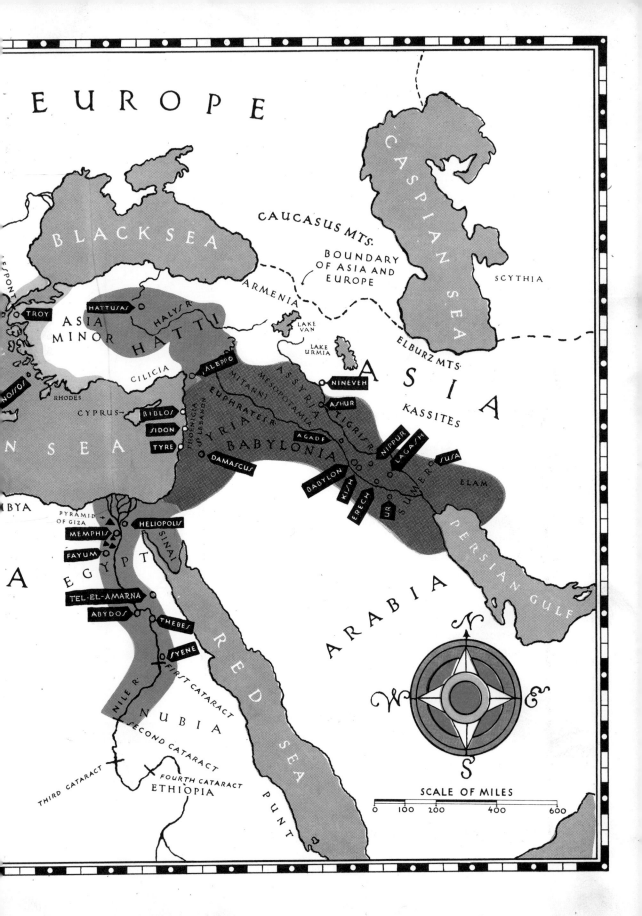

EUROPE

BLACK SEA

CAUCASUS MTS.

BOUNDARY
OF ASIA AND
EUROPE

CASPIAN SEA

SCYTHIA

ARMENIA

HELLESPONT

TROY

ASIA
MINOR

HATTUSAS

HATTI

HALYS R.

LAKE
VAN

LAKE
URMIA

ELBURZ MTS.

CILICIA

ALEPPO

MITANNI

MESOPOTAMIA

ASSYRIA

NINEVEH

ASHUR

KASSITES

ASIA

KNOSSOS

RHODES

CYPRUS

BIBLOS

SIDON

TYRE

PHOENICIA

MT. LEBANON

EUPHRATES R.

SYRIA

BABYLONIA

AGADE

TIGRIS R.

NIPPUR

LAGASH

SUSA

ELAM

SEA

DAMASCUS

BABYLON

KISH

ERECH

UR

SUMER

PERSIAN GULF

LIBYA

PYRAMID
OF GIZA

HELIOPOLIS

MEMPHIS

FAYUM

EGYPT

SINAI

ARABIA

N

W   E

S

A

TEL-EL-AMARNA

ABYDOS

THEBES

RED SEA

SYENE

FIRST CATARACT

NILE R.

NUBIA

SECOND CATARACT

THIRD CATARACT

FOURTH CATARACT

ETHIOPIA

PUNT

SCALE OF MILES

0   100   200   400   600

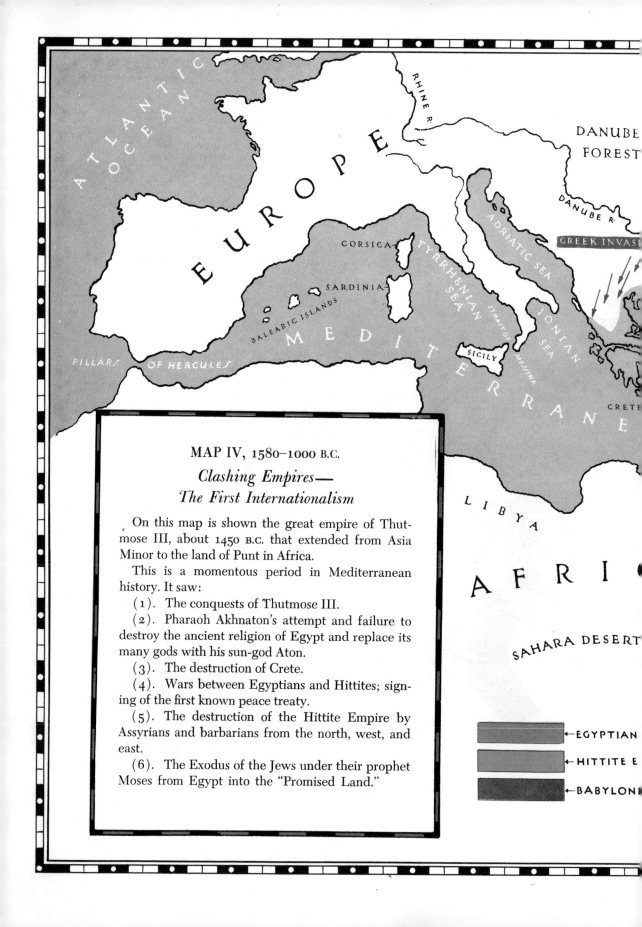

ATLANTIC OCEAN

RHINE R.

DANUBE FOREST

DANUBE R.

EUROPE

GREEK INVAS

ADRIATIC SEA

CORSICA

SARDINIA

TYRRHENIAN SEA

IONIAN SEA

STRAITS OF MESSINA

BALEARIC ISLANDS

SICILY

CRETE

MEDITERRANE

PILLARS OF HERCULES

LIBYA

AFRIC

MAP IV, 1580–1000 B.C.

Clashing Empires—
The First Internationalism

On this map is shown the great empire of Thutmose III, about 1450 B.C. that extended from Asia Minor to the land of Punt in Africa.

This is a momentous period in Mediterranean history. It saw:

(1). The conquests of Thutmose III.

(2). Pharaoh Akhnaton's attempt and failure to destroy the ancient religion of Egypt and replace its many gods with his sun-god Aton.

(3). The destruction of Crete.

(4). Wars between Egyptians and Hittites; signing of the first known peace treaty.

(5). The destruction of the Hittite Empire by Assyrians and barbarians from the north, west, and east.

(6). The Exodus of the Jews under their prophet Moses from Egypt into the "Promised Land."

SAHARA DESERT

←EGYPTIAN

←HITTITE E

←BABYLON

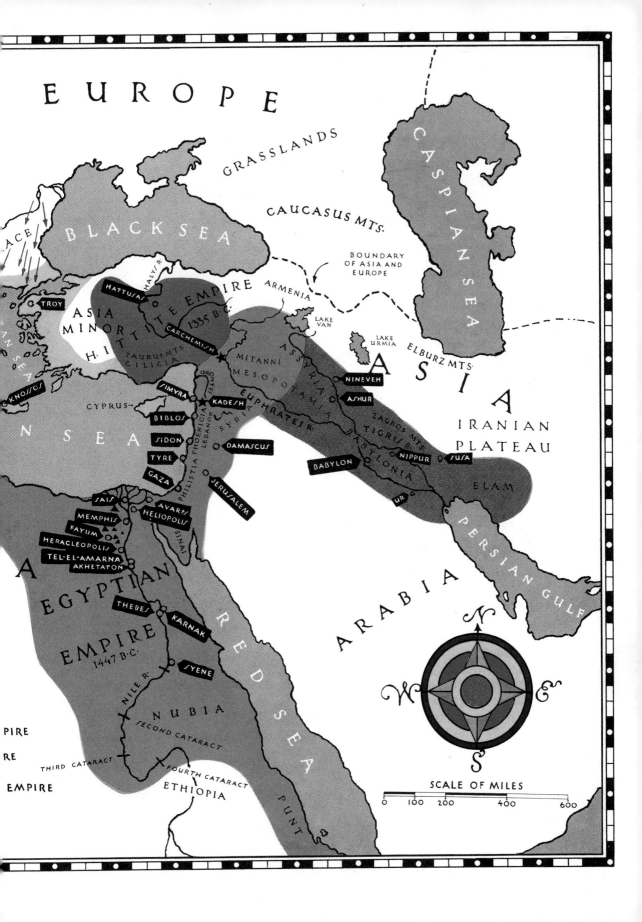

EUROPE

GRASSLANDS

CAUCASUS MTS.

BLACK SEA

CASPIAN SEA

BOUNDARY
OF ASIA AND
EUROPE

ARMENIA

TROY

HALYS R.

ASIA
MINOR

HATTUSAS

HITTITE EMPIRE

1335 B.C.

CARCHEMISH

LAKE
VAN

LAKE
URMIA

MITANNI

TAURUS MTS
CILICIA

HITT

ORO

MESOPOTAMIA

ASSYRIA

ELBURZ MTS.

ASIA

NINEVEH

ASHUR

IRANIAN
PLATEAU

KNOSSOS

SIMYRA

EUPHRATES R.

SYRIA

ZAGROS MTS

CYPRUS

SEA

BIBLOS

SIDON

TYRE

GAZA

KADESH

DAMASCUS

PHOENICIA

LEBANON

TIGRIS R.

BABYLONIA

NIPPUR

SUSA

BABYLON

ELAM

JERUSALEM

SAIS

AVARIS

PHILISTIA

UR

MEMPHIS

FAYUM

HELIOPOLIS

HERACLEOPOLIS

TEL-EL-AMARNA
AKHETATON

SINAI

PIRE

RE

A

EGYPTIAN

ARABIA

PERSIAN GULF

EMPIRE
1447 B.C.

THEBES

KARNAK

RED SEA

N

W   E

EMPIRE

SYENE

NILE R.

NUBIA

SECOND CATARACT

THIRD CATARACT

FOURTH CATARACT

ETHIOPIA

PUNT

S

SCALE OF MILES

0   100   200   400   600

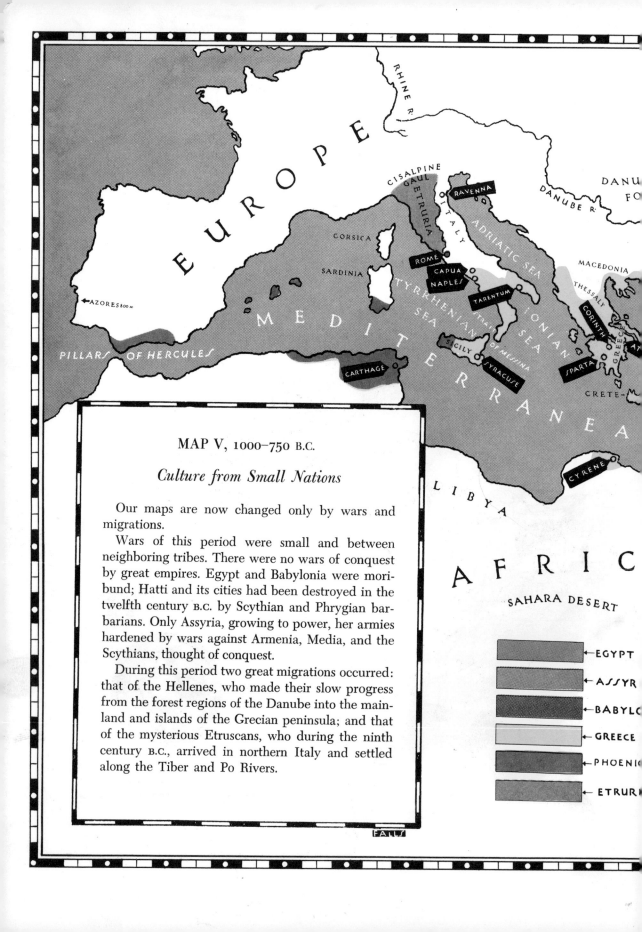

RHINE R.

EUROPE

DANU
FO

CISALPINE
GAUL

DANUBE R.

ETRURIA

RAVENNA

ITALY

ADRIATIC SEA

CORSICA

MACEDONIA

SARDINIA

ROME

THESSALY

CAPUA
NAPLES

TYRRHENIAN SEA

←AZORES 800 M

TARENTUM

IONIAN SEA

CORINTH

GREECE

M   E   D   I   T   E   R   R   A   N   E   A

SICILY

STRAIT OF MESSINA

SPARTA

AT

PILLARS OF HERCULES

SYRACUSE

CRETE

CARTHAGE

CYRENE

LIBYA

MAP V, 1000–750 B.C.

Culture from Small Nations

Our maps are now changed only by wars and
migrations.

Wars of this period were small and between
neighboring tribes. There were no wars of conquest
by great empires. Egypt and Babylonia were mori-
bund; Hatti and its cities had been destroyed in the
twelfth century B.C. by Scythian and Phrygian barbarians. Only Assyria, growing to power, her armies
hardened by wars against Armenia, Media, and the
Scythians, thought of conquest.

During this period two great migrations occurred:
that of the Hellenes, who made their slow progress
from the forest regions of the Danube into the mainland and islands of the Grecian peninsula; and that
of the mysterious Etruscans, who during the ninth
century B.C., arrived in northern Italy and settled
along the Tiber and Po Rivers.

AFRIC

SAHARA DESERT

←EGYPT

←ASSYR

←BABYLO

←GREECE

←PHOENIC

←ETRUR

FALLS

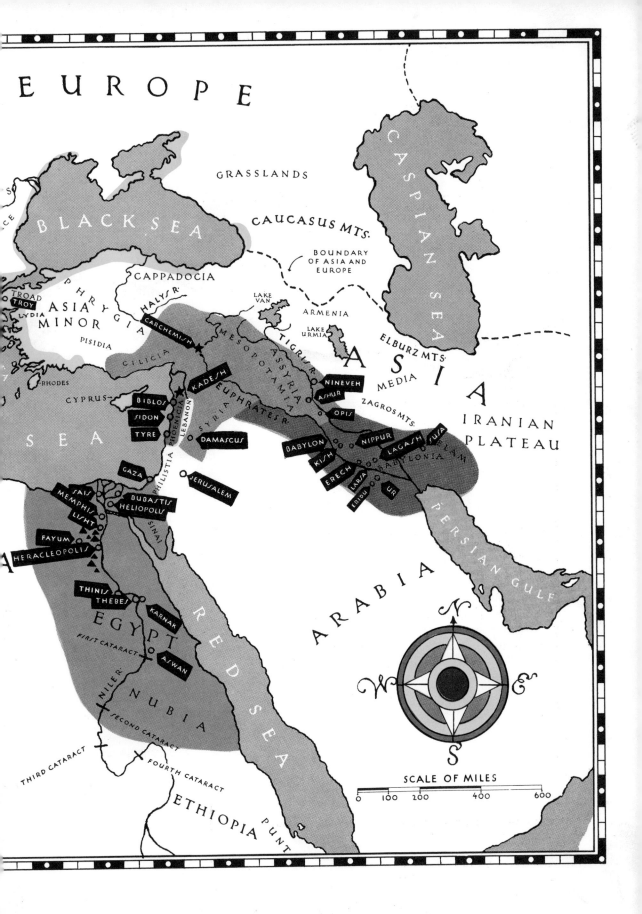

EUROPE

GRASSLANDS

CAUCASUS MTS.

CASPIAN SEA

BOUNDARY
OF ASIA AND
EUROPE

BLACK SEA

CAPPADOCIA

PHRYGIA

HALYS R.

LAKE
VAN

ARMENIA

TROAD
TROY
LYDIA

ASIA
MINOR

CARCHEMISH

MESOPOTAMIA

TIGRIS R.

ASSYRIA

LAKE
URMIA

ELBURZ MTS.

MEDIA

ASIA

PISIDIA

CILICIA

KADESH

EUPHRATES R.

SYRIA

NINEVEH
ASHUR

ZAGROS MTS.

IRANIAN
PLATEAU

RHODES

CYPRUS

BIBLOS

SIDON

TYRE

LEBANON

PHOENICIA

DAMASCUS

OPIS

BABYLON

NIPPUR

LAGASH

SUSA

ELAM

SEA

GAZA

PHILISTIA

JERUSALEM

KISH

ERECH

LARSA

BABYLONIA

URU

SAIS
MEMPHIS
LISHT

BUBASTIS
HELIOPOLIS

ERIDU

FAYUM

SINAI

HERACLEOPOLIS

ARABIA

PERSIAN GULF

THINIS
THEBES

KARNAK

EGYPT

N

FIRST CATARACT

ASWAN

W

E

NILE R.

NUBIA

RED SEA

S

SECOND CATARACT

SCALE OF MILES

THIRD CATARACT

FOURTH CATARACT

0   100   200   400   600

ETHIOPIA

PUNT

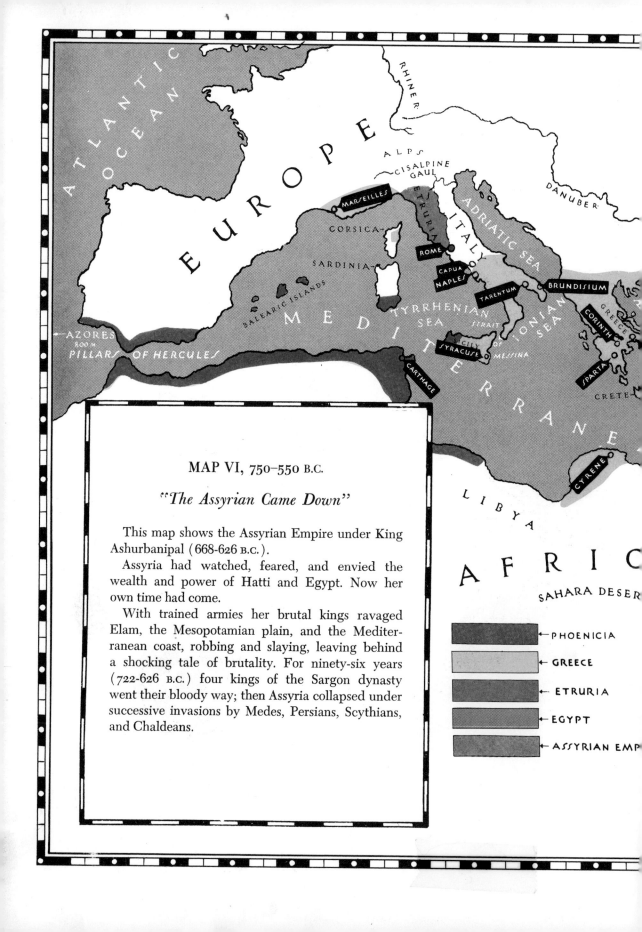

ATLANTIC OCEAN

EUROPE

RHINE R.

ALPS

CISALPINE GAUL

DANUBE R.

MARSEILLES

CORSICA

ETRURIA

ITALY

ADRIATIC SEA

SARDINIA

ROME

CAPUA

NAPLES

BALEARIC ISLANDS

TARENTUM

BRUNDISIUM

GREECE

CORINTH

MEDITERRANEAN

TYRRHENIAN SEA

STRAIT OF MESSINA

SICILY

IONIAN SEA

SPARTA

SYRACUSE

CRETE

AZORES 800 M.

PILLARS OF HERCULES

CARTHAGE

CYRENE

LIBYA

AFRIC

SAHARA DESER

MAP VI, 750–550 B.C.

"The Assyrian Came Down"

This map shows the Assyrian Empire under King Ashurbanipal (668-626 B.C.).

Assyria had watched, feared, and envied the wealth and power of Hatti and Egypt. Now her own time had come.

With trained armies her brutal kings ravaged Elam, the Mesopotamian plain, and the Mediterranean coast, robbing and slaying, leaving behind a shocking tale of brutality. For ninety-six years (722-626 B.C.) four kings of the Sargon dynasty went their bloody way; then Assyria collapsed under successive invasions by Medes, Persians, Scythians, and Chaldeans.

← PHOENICIA

← GREECE

← ETRURIA

← EGYPT

← ASSYRIAN EMP

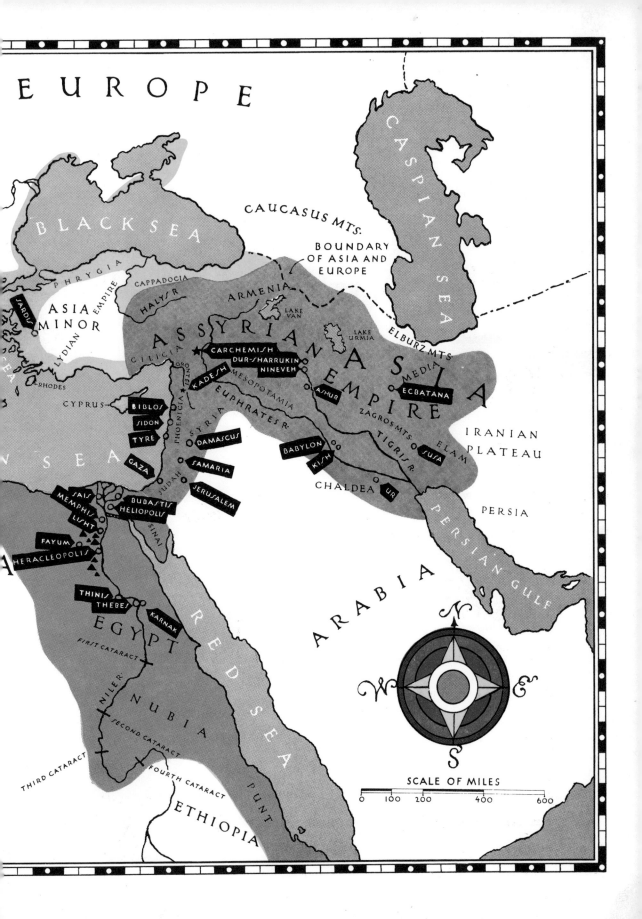

EUROPE

BLACK SEA

CAUCASUS MTS.

BOUNDARY
OF ASIA AND
EUROPE

CASPIAN SEA

PHRYGIA

CAPPADOCIA

ARMENIA

LAKE
VAN

LAKE
URMIA

ELBURZ MTS

ASIA
MINOR

SARDIS

LYDIAN EMPIRE

HALYS R.

CILICIA

ASSYRIAN

ASIA

MEDIA

ECBATANA

EMPIRE

RHODES

CYPRUS

CARCHEMISH
DUR-SHARRUKIN
NINEVEH

KADESH

ORONTES R.

MESOPOTAMIA

ASHUR

EUPHRATES R.

ZAGROS MTS.

IRANIAN
PLATEAU

BIBLOS
SIDON

PHOENICIA

SYRIA

TIGRIS R.

ELAM

SUSA

TYRE

DAMASCUS

BABYLON

KISH

GAZA

SAMARIA

JUDAH

CHALDEA

UR

PERSIA

SAIS
MEMPHIS
LISHT

BUBASTIS
HELIOPOLIS

JERUSALEM

FAYUM

HERACLEOPOLIS

SINAI

ARABIA

PERSIAN GULF

THINIS
THEBES

KARNAK

EGYPT

FIRST CATARACT

RED SEA

NILE R.

NUBIA

SECOND CATARACT

N

THIRD CATARACT

FOURTH CATARACT

W   E

PUNT

S

ETHIOPIA

SCALE OF MILES

0   100   200   400   600

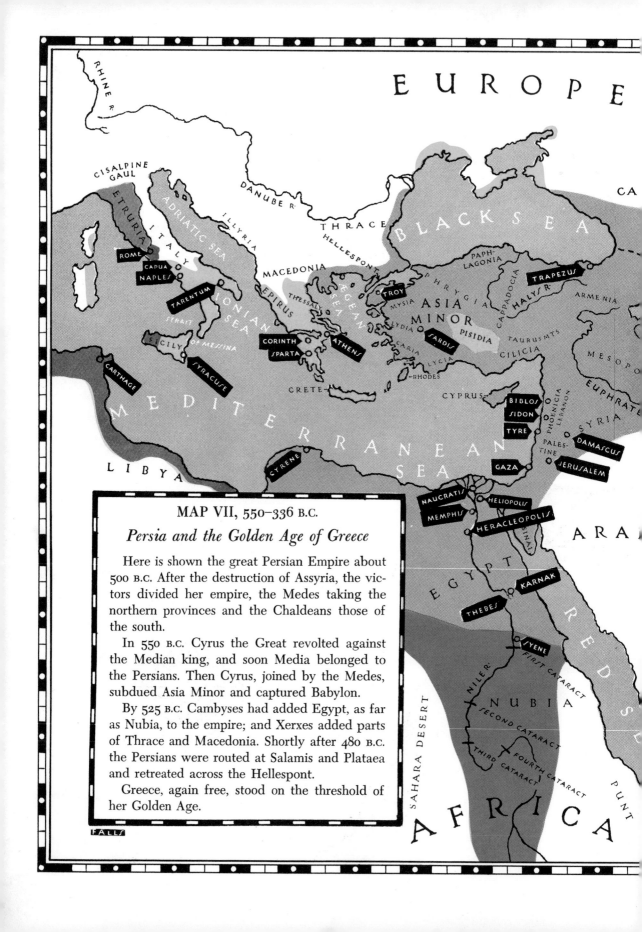

MAP VII, 550–336 B.C.

Persia and the Golden Age of Greece

Here is shown the great Persian Empire about 500 B.C. After the destruction of Assyria, the victors divided her empire, the Medes taking the northern provinces and the Chaldeans those of the south.

In 550 B.C. Cyrus the Great revolted against the Median king, and soon Media belonged to the Persians. Then Cyrus, joined by the Medes, subdued Asia Minor and captured Babylon.

By 525 B.C. Cambyses had added Egypt, as far as Nubia, to the empire; and Xerxes added parts of Thrace and Macedonia. Shortly after 480 B.C. the Persians were routed at Salamis and Plataea and retreated across the Hellespont.

Greece, again free, stood on the threshold of her Golden Age.

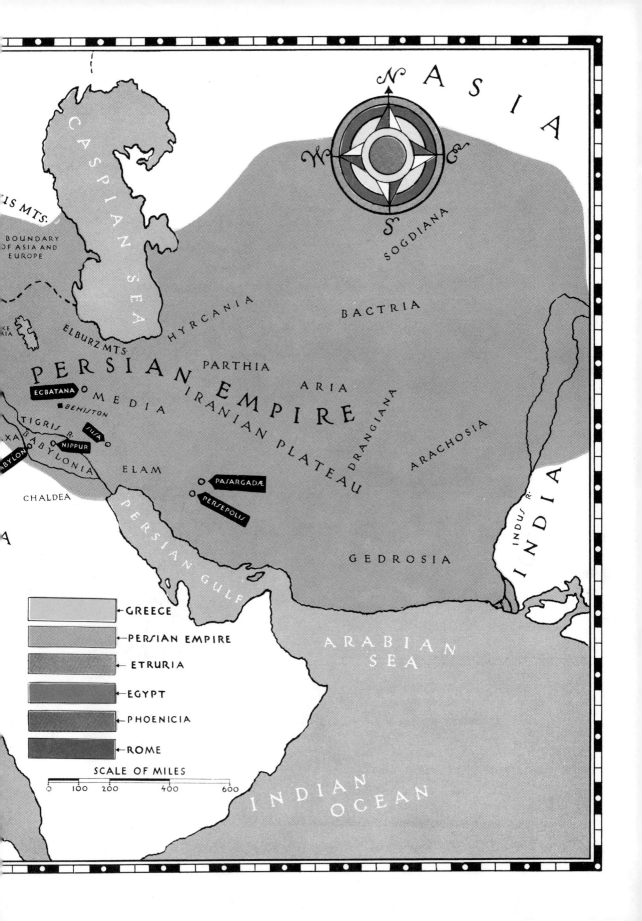

ASIA

CASPIAN SEA

SOGDIANA

BOUNDARY
OF ASIA AND
EUROPE

COLCHIS MTS.

HYRCANIA

BACTRIA

ELBURZ MTS.

PARTHIA

PERSIAN EMPIRE

ARIA

ECBATANA

MEDIA

BEHISTON

IRANIAN PLATEAU

DRANGIANA

ARACHOSIA

TIGRIS R.

SUSA

BABYLON

NIPPUR

BABYLONIA

ELAM

PASARGADÆ

INDIA

PERSEPOLIS

INDUS R.

CHALDEA

PERSIAN GULF

GEDROSIA

ARABIAN
SEA

GREECE

PERSIAN EMPIRE

ETRURIA

EGYPT

PHOENICIA

ROME

SCALE OF MILES

0   100   200   400   600

INDIAN   OCEAN

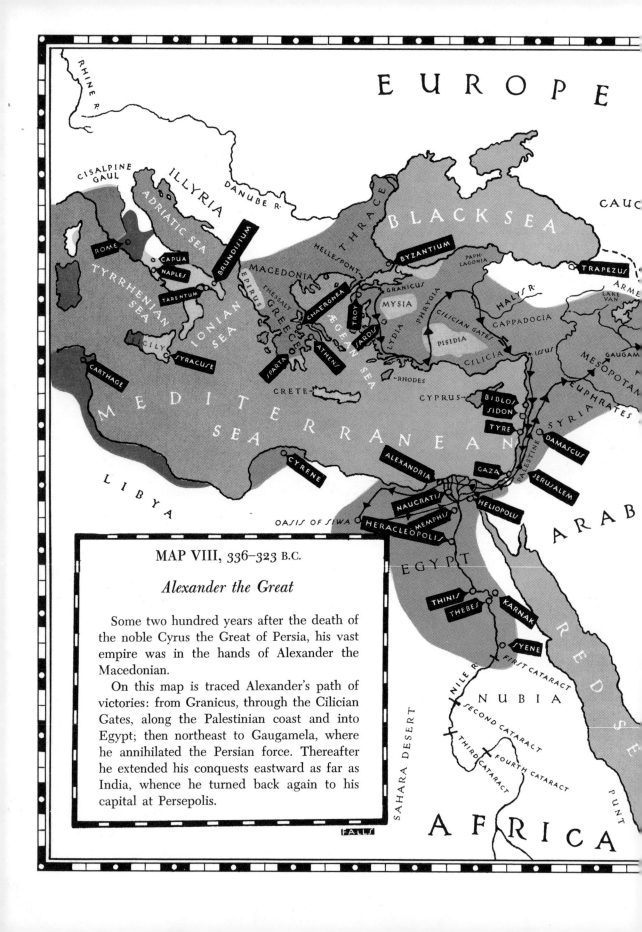

EUROPE

RHINE R.

CISALPINE GAUL
ILLYRIA
DANUBE R.
ADRIATIC SEA
ROME
CAPUA
NAPLES
BRUNDISIUM
TYRRHENIAN SEA
TARENTUM
MACEDONIA
EPIRUS
THESSALY
GREECE
CHAERONEA
TROY
SARDIS
SPARTA
ATHENS
AEGEAN SEA
CILY
SYRACUSE
IONIAN SEA
EUBOEA
CRETE
RHODES

BLACK SEA
THRACE
BYZANTIUM
PAPH-LAGONIA
TRAPEZUS
HELLESPONT
GRANICUS
MYSIA
PHRYGIA
LYDIA
CILICIAN GATES
PISIDIA
CILICIA
CAPPADOCIA
HALYS R.
ISSUS
ARME
LAKE VAN
CAUC
GAUGAM
MESOPOTAM
EUPHRATES

CYPRUS
BIBLOS
SIDON
TYRE
DAMASCUS
SYRIA

CARTHAGE
MEDITERRANEAN SEA
CYRENE
ALEXANDRIA
GAZA
JERUSALEM
PALESTINE

LIBYA
NAUCRATIS
HELIOPOLIS
HERACLEOPOLIS
MEMPHIS
OASIS OF SIWA

ARAB

EGYPT

THINIS
THEBES
KARNAK
SYENE
FIRST CATARACT

NILE R.
SAHARA DESERT
NUBIA
SECOND CATARACT
THIRD CATARACT
FOURTH CATARACT
PUNT
RED SEA

AFRICA

MAP VIII, 336–323 B.C.

Alexander the Great

Some two hundred years after the death of
the noble Cyrus the Great of Persia, his vast
empire was in the hands of Alexander the
Macedonian.

On this map is traced Alexander's path of
victories: from Granicus, through the Cilician
Gates, along the Palestinian coast and into
Egypt; then northeast to Gaugamela, where
he annihilated the Persian force. Thereafter
he extended his conquests eastward as far as
India, whence he turned back again to his
capital at Persepolis.

FALLS

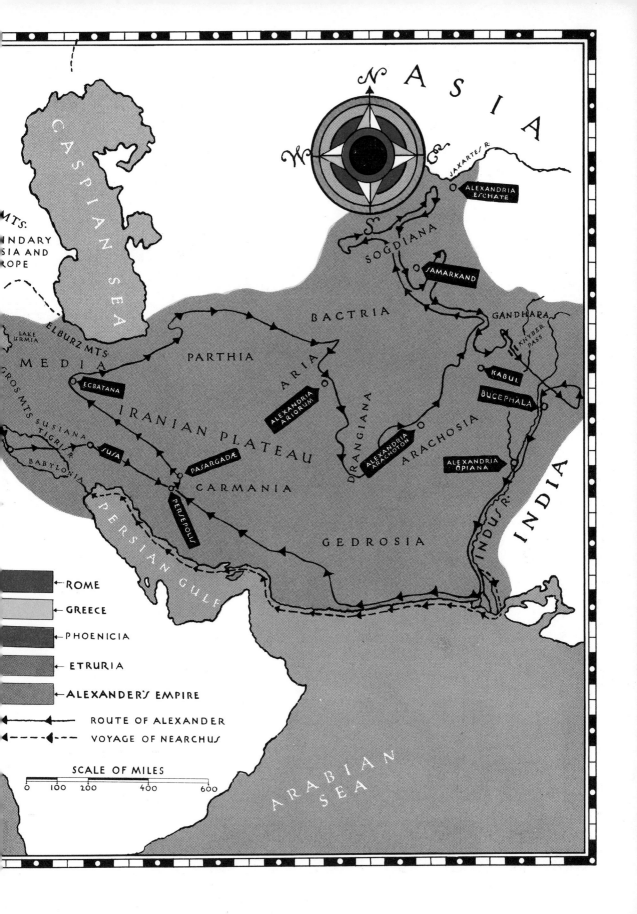

N A S I A

JAXARTES R.

ALEXANDRIA
ESCHATE

SOGDIANA

SAMARKAND

GANDHARA

CASPIAN SEA

MTS.
NDARY
SIA AND
ROPE

ELBURZ MTS.

LAKE
URMIA

BACTRIA

KNYBER
PASS

MEDIA

PARTHIA

ARIA

KABUL

BUCEPHALA

ECBATANA

IRANIAN PLATEAU

ALEXANDRIA
ARIORUM

DRANGIANA

ALEXANDRIA
OPIANA

ROS MTS.

SUSIANA
TIGRIS R.

SUSA

PASARGADÆ

ALEXANDRIA
ARACHOTON

ARACHOSIA

INDUS R.

INDIA

BABYLONIA

PERSEPOLIS

CARMANIA

PERSIAN GULF

GEDROSIA

ROME

GREECE

PHOENICIA

ETRURIA

ALEXANDER'S EMPIRE

ROUTE OF ALEXANDER

VOYAGE OF NEARCHUS

SCALE OF MILES

0   100   200   400   600

ARABIAN
SEA

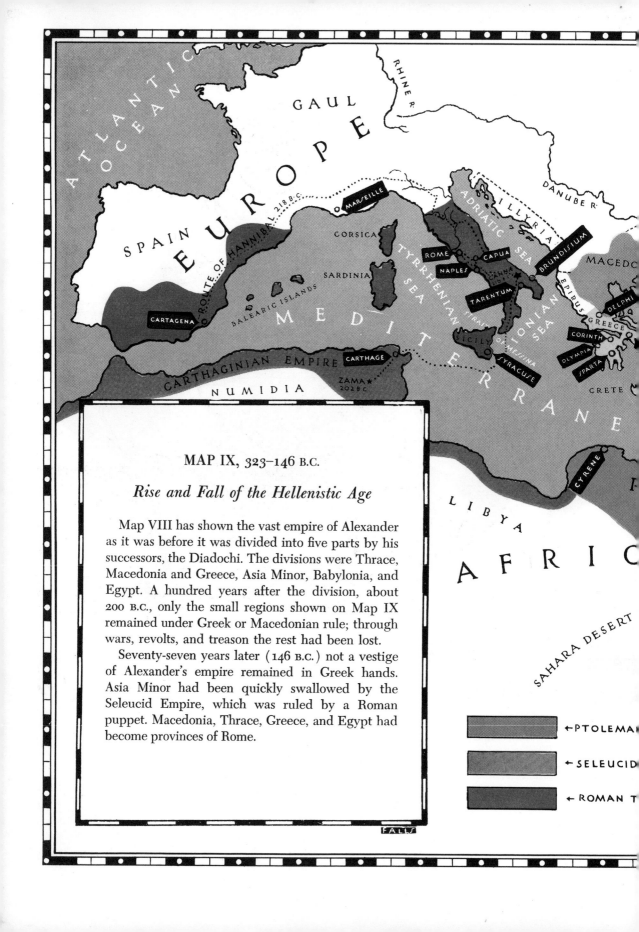

ATLANTIC OCEAN

GAUL

RHINE R.

DANUBE R.

SPAIN

EUROPE

ROUTE OF HANNIBAL 218 B.C.

MARSEILLE

CORSICA

SARDINIA

BALEARIC ISLANDS

TYRRHENIAN SEA

ILLYRIA

ADRIATIC SEA

ROME

NAPLES

CAPUA

CANNAE 216 BC

BRUNDISIUM

MACEDO

EPIRUS

TARENTUM

DELPHI

GREECE

CORINTH

OLYMPIA

SPARTA

CRETE

MEDITERRANEAN

STRAIT OF MESSINA

SICILY

SYRACUSE

IONIAN SEA

CARTAGENA

CARTHAGINIAN EMPIRE

CARTHAGE

NUMIDIA

ZAMA ★
202 B.C.

MAP IX, 323–146 B.C.

Rise and Fall of the Hellenistic Age

Map VIII has shown the vast empire of Alexander as it was before it was divided into five parts by his successors, the Diadochi. The divisions were Thrace, Macedonia and Greece, Asia Minor, Babylonia, and Egypt. A hundred years after the division, about 200 B.C., only the small regions shown on Map IX remained under Greek or Macedonian rule; through wars, revolts, and treason the rest had been lost.

Seventy-seven years later (146 B.C.) not a vestige of Alexander's empire remained in Greek hands. Asia Minor had been quickly swallowed by the Seleucid Empire, which was ruled by a Roman puppet. Macedonia, Thrace, Greece, and Egypt had become provinces of Rome.

LIBYA

AFRIC

SAHARA DESERT

CYRENE

←PTOLEMA

←SELEUCID

←ROMAN T

FALLS

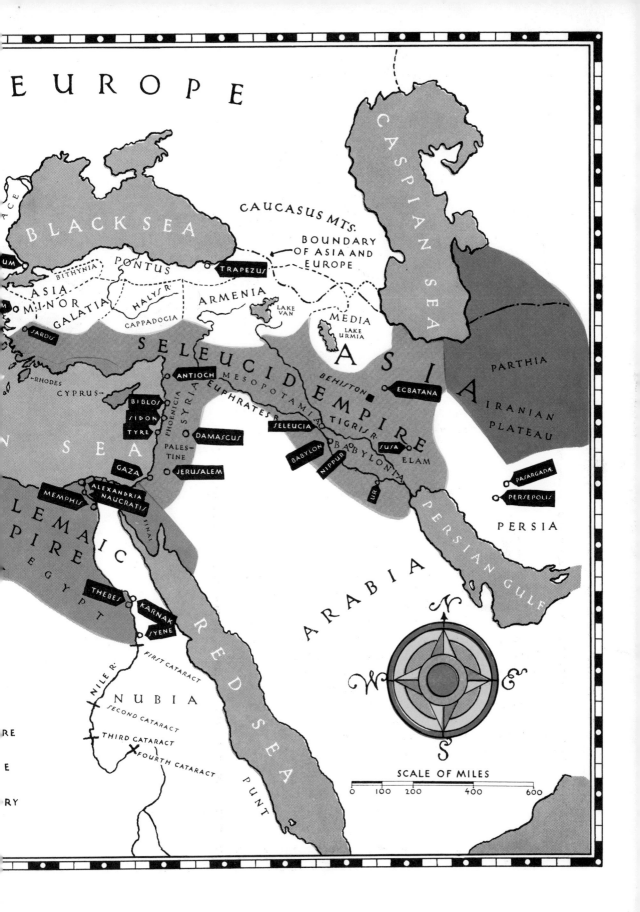

EUROPE

BLACK SEA

CAUCASUS MTS.
BOUNDARY
OF ASIA AND
EUROPE

CASPIAN SEA

BITHYNIA
PONTUS
TRAPEZUS
ASIA
MINOR
GALATIA
HALYS R.
CAPPADOCIA
ARMENIA
LAKE VAN
MEDIA
LAKE URMIA

A S I A

PARTHIA

IRANIAN
PLATEAU

SARDIS

RHODES
CYPRUS

SELEUCID EMPIRE
ANTIOCH
MESOPOTAMIA
EUPHRATES R.
SYRIA
BEHISTUN
TIGRIS R.
ECBATANA

BIBLOS
SIDON
TYRE
PHOENICIA
SELEUCIA
SUSA
ELAM

DAMASCUS
PALES-
TINE
BABYLON
NIPPUR
BABYLONIA

PASARGADAE
PERSEPOLIS

N SEA
GAZA
JERUSALEM
UR

PERSIA

MEMPHIS
ALEXANDRIA
NAUCRATIS

SINAI

PERSIAN GULF

LEMAIC
PIRE
EGYPT

ARABIA

THEBES
KARNAK
SYENE

RED SEA

NILE R.
FIRST CATARACT

NUBIA
SECOND CATARACT
THIRD CATARACT
FOURTH CATARACT

PUNT

N
W   E
S

SCALE OF MILES
0   100   200   400   600

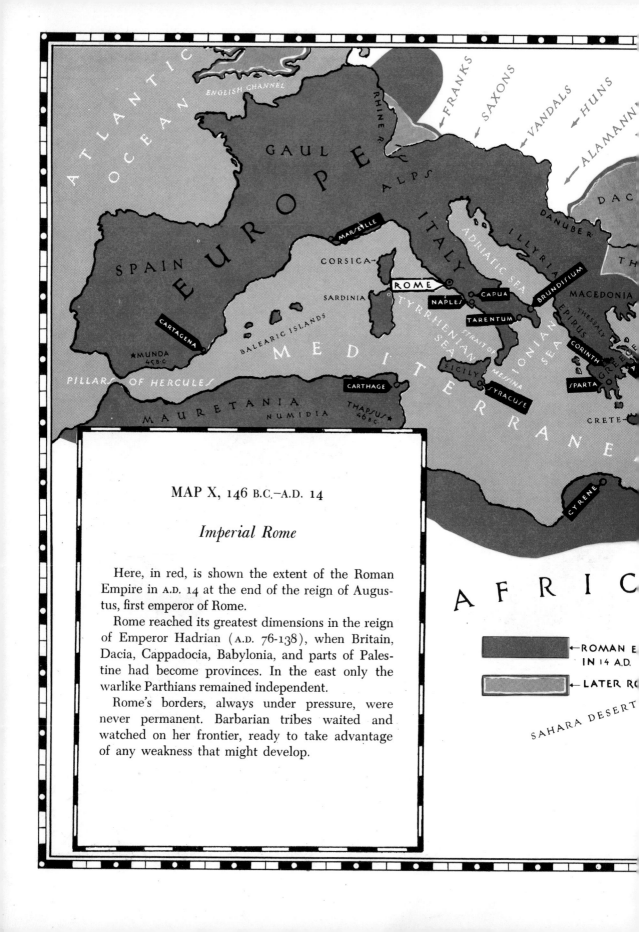

ATLANTIC OCEAN

ENGLISH CHANNEL

EUROPE

GAUL

SPAIN

ALPS

RHINE R.

FRANKS

SAXONS

VANDALS

HUNS

ALAMANN

DANUBE R.

DAC

ILLYRIA

MACEDONIA

TH

THESSALY

EPIRUS

CORINTH

SPARTA

GREECE

MARSEILLE

CORSICA

SARDINIA

BALEARIC ISLANDS

ROME

NAPLES

CAPUA

TARENTUM

BRUNDISIUM

ITALY

ADRIATIC SEA

TYRRHENIAN SEA

IONIAN SEA

STRAIT OF MESSINA

SICILY

SYRACUSE

CARTAGENA

★MUNDA 45 B.C.

PILLARS OF HERCULES

CARTHAGE

MAURETANIA

NUMIDIA

THAPSUS 46 B.C.★

MEDITERRANE

CRETE

CYRENE

AFRIC

SAHARA DESERT

MAP X, 146 B.C.–A.D. 14

Imperial Rome

Here, in red, is shown the extent of the Roman Empire in A.D. 14 at the end of the reign of Augustus, first emperor of Rome.

Rome reached its greatest dimensions in the reign of Emperor Hadrian (A.D. 76-138), when Britain, Dacia, Cappadocia, Babylonia, and parts of Palestine had become provinces. In the east only the warlike Parthians remained independent.

Rome's borders, always under pressure, were never permanent. Barbarian tribes waited and watched on her frontier, ready to take advantage of any weakness that might develop.

ROMAN E
IN 14 A.D.

LATER R

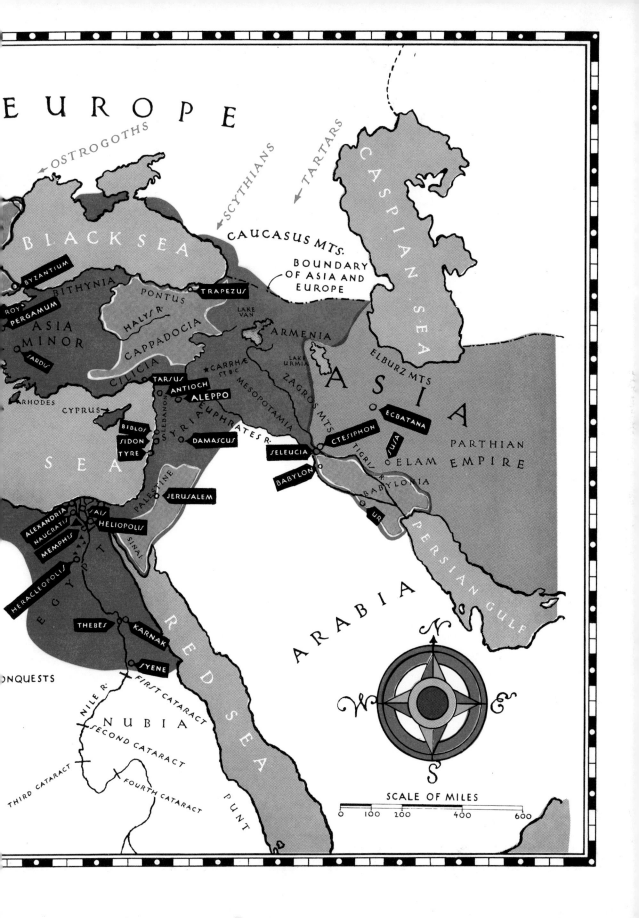

EUROPE

OSTROGOTHS

SCYTHIANS

TARTARS

CAUCASUS MTS.

BOUNDARY
OF ASIA AND
EUROPE

CASPIAN SEA

BLACK SEA

BYZANTIUM

BITHYNIA

ROY.

PERGAMUM

ASIA
MINOR

SARDIS

RHODES

CYPRUS

PONTUS

HALYS R.

CAPPADOCIA

CILICIA

TARSUS

ANTIOCH

ALEPPO

BIBLOS

SIDON

TYRE

DAMASCUS

LEBANON

SYRIA

EUPHRATES R.

MESOPOTAMIA

TRAPEZUS

LAKE
VAN

ARMENIA

LAKE
URMIA

★CARRHÆ
53 B.C.

ZAGROS MTS.

ELBURZ MTS

ASIA

ECBATANA

SEA

PALESTINE

JERUSALEM

ALEXANDRIA

NAUCRATIS

SAIS

HELIOPOLIS

MEMPHIS

HERACLEOPOLIS

EGYPT

THEBES

KARNAK

SYENE

SINAI

SELEUCIA

BABYLON

CTESIPHON

TIGRIS R.

SUSA

ELAM

BABYLONIA

UR

PARTHIAN
EMPIRE

PERSIAN GULF

ARABIA

RED SEA

CONQUESTS

NILE R.

FIRST CATARACT

NUBIA

SECOND CATARACT

THIRD CATARACT

FOURTH CATARACT

PUNT

N

W   E

S

SCALE OF MILES

0   100   200   400   600

The First 3000 Years:
ANCIENT CIVILIZATIONS OF THE TIGRIS, EUPHRATES, AND NILE RIVER VALLEYS, AND THE MEDITERRANEAN SEA

SUMERIAN CHARIOT

This four-wheeled Sumerian chariot is drawn by onagers (wild asses).
In it rides Mes-Kalam-Shar, a prince of Ur, wearing a golden helmet.
An attendant drives, and four guards serve as royal escort. Our data
for this scene come from the so-called "Standard of Ur"—a mosaic
depicting peace and war, discovered in a royal tomb by the English
archaeologist Sir Leonard Woolley.

I.   Two Valleys

4000-3000 B. C.

Mediterranean civilization began in two great river valleys—the valley
of the Nile, and the valley of the Euphrates, the river of Paradise.

Ancient people believed that the Nile flowed from a heavenly river
on which the sun god's bark daily crossed the skies. Not till modern
times did man solve the mystery of the sources of the Nile. It is really
two rivers at first. The White Nile rises in the heart of Africa and flows
northward for the better part of three thousand miles, till it is joined by

39

the Blue Nile that rises in Ethiopia. Hundreds of miles beyond the meeting of the rivers is the First Cataract.

From there the Nile flows in slow majesty through its narrow valley, only twelve to thirty-one miles wide, between high yellow and strawberry-red sandstone cliffs. A hundred miles from the Mediterranean it forms a swampy delta and many mouths empty its brown flood into the sea. In the fabulous strip of territory, stretching some seven hundred and fifty miles between the First Cataract and the Mediterranean, the ancient kingdom of Egypt flourished under the blazing African sun.

The Nile was Egypt's highway and the source of its life. Each year the spring rains of central Africa combined with snow water from the mountains of Ethiopia and caused the river to overflow its banks. By June the flood reached the valley, spreading silt over it and renewing its fertility. Along this beautiful and productive land, prehistoric men wandered for thousands of years; their stone implements have been found there. And here a great civilization began.

Its "form" and history were shaped by the annual miracle of the Nile and the unique setting of the valley. Along that single life-giving river, an industrious people joined into a monolithic union under a semi-divine Pharaoh. Nor had they any invaders to fear. To the east lay the desolate Red Sea; to the west, the wastes of the Sahara Desert; to the south was Nubia, a wilderness then occupied by primitive Negro tribes. Egypt, therefore, was protected from three sides. Only from the north would her conquerors eventually come, from Asia across the Isthmus of Suez, from Libya just west of the Delta. So for long centuries Egypt was secure in the valley of the Nile, destined to develop her culture in unity and peace.

But neither peace nor unity awaited the Biblical land where the great civilization of Sumer arose, the valley of the Tigris and Euphrates Rivers. Four names have been given that region—the Land Between the Two Rivers, Mesopotamia (which means the same thing in Greek), and for the southerly portion, the Plain of Shinar, and the Plain of Babylon. Most intriguing of all, the Bible says that the Euphrates is the river that watered Paradise!

Be that as it may, the Tigris and Euphrates both rise in the mountains of Asia Minor, then twist and turn to flow more than fifteen hundred miles southeast through the valley, till they empty their turgid waters into the Persian Gulf. Every year a spring flood brings alluvial silt from the north to fertilize the land, as it does with the Nile. These floods, however, are treacherous: high tides in the Gulf and southerly gales, sudden snowstorms and rainstorms and landslides in gorges to the north—any of them may cause a local rush of river water, a crumbling of mud embankments, a shifting of channels. But here, too, have been found the remains of prehistoric cultures: painted pottery, chipped flint, volcanic glass. They were buried under a layer of pure clay eight feet thick, the remains of a great flood—possibly the Flood which Noah survived in the Ark.

For it was probably from Sumerian records, by way of Babylon, that the traditional stories of the Creation, the Garden of Eden, and the Flood reached the Bible. And the first great epic—the story of the Sumerian demigod Gilgamesh, written on cuneiform tablets—tells a strangely familiar tale: Uta-Napisthim was warned by a god of the coming of the flood, and told to build a large boat to hold himself and a pair of every species of animal in the world. This he did. Rains brought the flood, and when the waters subsided all were saved.

In this fabled and turbulent land, a very different civilization developed through centuries of war and turmoil. Here arose the ancient temple communities of Sumer—the first cities in the world—achieving local brilliance on their shifting rivers, but warring endlessly with one another. And their fertile plain at the gateway to the Near East lay open to all invaders. Conquest followed conquest, nation followed nation: Sumer, Akkad, Babylon, Assyria. Indo-European and Semite have fought each other in this land down to the present day. While the Nile Valley was enjoying its long chronicle of peace, the plain watered by the River of Paradise was a battleground for endless wars.

EARLY EGYPT

Egypt's early history was literally dug up from the desert sands and the Delta mud by order of Napoleon Bonaparte! When Napoleon invaded the land of the Nile in A.D. 1798 he took with him two armies. There were regiments of soldiers, of course, but the military adventure failed. He had, however, another company of artists, scholars, and scientists who had come to study and picture the ancient civilization of Egypt. And the scientific side of the invasion was a magnificent success: it brought a brilliant culture back to life for the world.

On that expedition a French soldier, digging a trench near the Rosetta mouth of the Nile, made a great find. He unearthed an oblong stone of black basalt with broken corners, twenty-eight and a half inches wide and forty-five inches high, covered all over by inscriptions. It was what scholars call a trilingual—that is, a record with the same text inscribed on it in three languages. This was the famous Rosetta Stone. Its text was in Egyptian hieroglyphics, or sacred writing; demotic, or Egyptian, script; and Greek. The scholars who could read the Greek found that it was a decree in honor of Pharaoh Ptolemy V. It had been composed by Egyptian priests of Memphis to thank the Pharaoh for benefits they had received from him.

Now many savants studied the Egyptian hieroglyphics but failed to solve them. It remained for a young French scholar, Jean François Champollion, to decipher the hieroglyphics after twenty years of patient study. Then, by comparing the demotic writing with the Greek and the hieroglyphics, it was not hard to read the demotic writing too. So the Egyptian language, lost since Roman times, was again known. With this knowledge we can read the carved inscriptions on the monuments, the written papyrus, the Book of the Dead, and the cartouches on the scarabs. Nearly everything written in Egyptian hieroglyphic or demotic script can now be read.

The Rosetta Stone, key to our knowledge of Egypt's history, is preserved in the British Museum. That recorded history, we now know, began around 3000 B. C., but Egyptian civilization really started during the millennium before. And it was quite literally (in the words of an ancient proverb) "the gift of the Nile."

During several thousand years, Stone Age men had lived along the Nile, in grass huts clustered on high sandy spurs. For in prehistoric times the river flowed through a great marsh. But, probably around 8000 B. C., the area began to grow drier—perhaps this stimulated the draining of swamps and social cooperation. Yet the birth of civilization was a gradual process, though the final steps may have been swifter. Primitive hunters and fishers turned more and more to farming; copper was used, and quartz was cut; there was trade in semi-precious stones up and down the valley and across the nearby deserts; the dead were buried in pit graves, and provided with pottery and tools and eye make-up for the afterlife. Meantime the villages became town-states or "nomes," which were eventually grouped into two kingdoms—the Delta or Lower Egypt, under a king with a red crown, the valley proper or Upper Egypt, under a king with a white crown.

The "legendary" history of Egypt had begun. We know only its outlines: the rulers are described as fabulous beings, midway between gods and men, but some have left monuments. At first Lower Egypt (near the brilliant early civilization of Asia) was dominant; next, Upper Egypt was independent and equally powerful; then from 3400 to 3200 B. C. the two kingdoms were continually at war. Finally, a powerful warrior-king of Upper Egypt—the "Menes" or Eternal One of legend—conquered the Delta and united the land once and for all, becoming the First Pharaoh of the First Dynasty, Lord of Upper and Lower Egypt, wearer of the Double Crown. All Egyptian rulers thenceforth bore a series of sacred and royal titles, but they came to be called Pharaoh or "Great House" from the place where they lived. From the reign of Menes till Egypt fell to the Persians in 525 B. C., twenty-six dynasties of Pharaohs were to rule through more than two thousand five hundred years.

THE FIRST PHARAOH

Menes, the founder of Egypt's First Dynasty, is shown wearing the white crown of Upper Egypt and leading his archers into battle. He finally conquered the land of the Delta, built his capital at Memphis, and became the first to wear the double crown as Pharaoh of Upper and Lower Egypt.

Most of the records of the first historic age have been lost, though hieroglyphic writing was used and probably papyrus paper. But only a few sun-dried brick ruins remain, and we have scant data on the eighteen rulers of the First and Second Dynasties. Nonetheless we know that the culture of early Egypt developed along two main lines—large-scale irrigation of her narrow land, and absolute organization of her people under the Pharaohs.

Life revolved around the cycle of the Nile. As no rain fell on the valley, except in the Delta, it was necessary to conserve the waters of the early flood. To do this the skillful Egyptians learned to build ditches and dikes, and big catch-basins and miles of canals, so they could irrigate the fertile soil in the dry season and reclaim still more land by bringing water clear to the desert hills.

Now their fields flourished, and oxen pulled their plows; their cattle gave meat and milk; donkeys were their beasts of burden. They ate bread, meat, fruit, vegetables, and honey; and they drank milk, beer, and wine. In this fertile Nile Valley, perhaps for the first time, man had plenty of food every year that the Nile flooded. When the flood of the Nile failed, which was seldom, there was famine. With its cultivated richness, Egypt generally thrived.

Like the flood of her great river, Egypt's people were also under rigid control. Her society was based on the labor of subservient masses.

SHADOOF

This is a "shadoof" or well sweep, being used on the Nile. Also found in Mesopotamia, the device is still used in both lands. Historians argue as to which country invented it. Here, Egyptian workers are raising buckets of river water and emptying them into irrigation trenches. Two men are hoeing and, as always, an overseer watches the job.

The peasant or *fellah* was a virtual serf, bound to the soil in fact or in law—toiling in his own small garden-patch, in the great fields of the nobles, and on all the vast public works of the state. He stood at the base of the social pyramid. The apex of that pyramid was the Pharaoh, who was considered a god, son of a god, and absolute monarch. In theory, at least, the Pharaoh controlled everything. An inscription of the Twelfth Dynasty extolls him in these words: "Adore the king! Enthrone him in your hearts! He makes Egypt green more than the great Nile; he is life! He is the one who creates all that is. The Begetter who causes mankind to exist!" In practice, to be sure, he was only the head of a vast system. Between the Pharaoh and the peasants were viziers, nobles, governors, priests, landowners, scribes, artists, artisans, and laborers. But there were no soldiers, for in its early history the land was without a professional standing army; palace guards and local authorities kept the peace.

During those first centuries in Egypt, religious as well as social conservatism made for permanence. Man lives by his beliefs. And the Egyptians believed that the gods controlled the heavens, as Pharaoh, the god-king, ruled the earth.

But curiously, their pantheon did not have a single ruler. Heavenly power was divided among a host of deities, many of whom kept the stamp of that first age.

They held onto innumerable primitive gods; we have records of some two thousand! The land was filled with temples, and the temples were filled with idols: from cosmic "high gods" to a bewildering array of major and minor divinities—Ptah, Sekhet, Anubis, Hathor, Nephthys, and so on—to planets, the moon, stars, rocks, chieftains, and many animals that were worshiped locally. These last were of prehistoric origin. When Egypt was a land of nomes, each had an animal on its standard as totem or god. In time, these totems turned into animal-headed deities. The ibis became Thoth, the bull of Memphis became Apis, the cat of Bubastis became Bast. And Amon eventually rose along with his city of Thebes—from a village god shown as a ram or goose to a "great god" in human form with two goose-feathers decorating his head and the ram as his sacrificial animal.

Thus, over the centuries, certain deities gained supremacy, though Egyptian religion was never systematized. One such was Ra—pronounced "ray"—the sun-god of the blue sky. Another was Osiris, lord of the fertility of the Nile, with his consort Isis, the great earth-mother, and their son Horus, the falcon-headed god of light. (And Seth, the rival god of darkness.) But only Pharaoh himself was consistently the great god: at different times he was identified as the falcon-lord Horus, as the sun-god Ra or the son of Amon-Ra, and as Osiris, the ruler of the dead and god of resurrection.

For the Egyptians also believed in immortality—an idea grasped from the annual rebirth of the Nile valley—and early developed an elaborate cult of the dead. They thought the body and soul would have to stand trial before the judgment of Osiris. Therefore, at death, if the man was noble or rich, his body was embalmed so that he might be ready for the judgment. Then it was entombed, and food and all the necessary things of this life were also placed in the tomb for his use while he waited to go to the next world. On the walls of the tombs of important persons, a complete pictorial account of the life of the buried man was often painted. Here were represented his wife, his children, his servants, his work, and his play. Prayers for the departed were written on the walls of his coffin, as well as blessings, charms, magic spells, incantations, and poems in praise of the gods. Thus surrounded, his soul went to Osiris and his body awaited the resurrection! That was the final form of the Osirian cult; at different times the notions and practices varied, and in the earliest age they were restricted to Pharaoh and those interred with him. Yet for Egypt as a whole, immortality always had a special meaning.

In this cult of death and burial, the Egyptian showed his belief that death was only the continuance of life, and life was something to enjoy. Food and drink, games, hunting, fishing, boating, and wrestling; his pets, monkeys, birds, dogs, and cats; his children's toys—

representations of all these tell of his joy in life. Under his warm sun, in his life-giving valley, the man of early Egypt was a happy man.

ANCIENT SUMER

Egyptology has been studied since the Napoleonic era, but the oldest civilization of the Mediterranean was unearthed only in our own times. It was just a few decades ago that a British savant broke into the stillness of a Sumerian tomb—to gaze in awe at dead royalty surrounded by heaps of dazzling treasure!

Sir Leonard Woolley was the first to discover the splendors of ancient Sumer. Between 1922 and 1934 he made excavations at the site of Ur, and uncovered the tombs of King A-Bar-Gi and Queen Shub-Ad of the First Dynasty. He found the king buried with three retainers, and in an adjoining vault there were sixty-two more—a body-guard of death. With the queen was a retinue of twenty-five men and women, two wagons, six oxen, and a chariot with two asses. There were no signs of violence or terror. It was a tableau of silence, with every figure set. Here were guards with helmets and spears, nobles in their official robes, and women in gala dresses of red wool, their heads adorned with black wigs and headdresses in the mode of the queen. They looked as though they had all taken poison, lain down, arranged their clothes, and died. About the dead were placed multifarious objects showing the art and wealth of Sumer: fluted cups and vases of gold, gaming boards, model boats, copper bulls, lyres, harps, and jewelry of every kind, from headdresses to rings. There were also vessels of alabaster and of marble, and bowls of obsidian and lapis lazuli. Other graves of kings and nobles were found after that. They all contained human sacrifices, and all had been robbed.

These were exciting finds. And more was learned from the exploration of half-buried cities and overgrown ruins. But much of our knowledge of this most ancient culture of the Mediterranean has come from still another source. Early in Sumer's history her people used clay tablets for keeping records. These were flat tiles of soft clay on which they scratched, with reed points, the symbols of an alphabet they had devised. The writing was read from right to left. At first the tablets were dried in the sun; later on they were baked in ovens. When hardened, they might be used as letters or stored as records.

For about three thousand years, throughout the Near East, the lives of nations and men were recorded on these stone-hard tablets, which resisted the damage of time, water, and fire. Thousands of them have been dug out of the dust of forgotten cities to reveal stories of infamy and achievement. Thousands are still to be dug. But already these tablets, and the ruins and treasures, tell us the tale of ancient Sumer.

Around 4500 B. C., prehistoric dwellers in the swampy land at the head of the Persian Gulf were changing their ways. Who they were or where they came from is still a mystery. But we know that they turned from hunting to agriculture. Cattle, sheep, and goats were domesticated; simple reed-and-mud huts were replaced by buildings of sun-dried bricks laid in mortar made of bitumen; the earliest kind of writing, proto-writing, was invented. But most important, they learned (as did the Egyptians) to dig ditches and build dikes and dams, to control the spring floods and save water for the dry season; only three and a half inches of rain fall in that land per year. And with irrigation came social development. The villages grew into towns, and the towns into real cities, each one invariably built around a *ziggurat* or massive tower of bricks, with a temple for the local god on top. This was the "urban revolution" of the fourth millennium B. C.—the historical dawn of Western civilization on the Mesopotamian plain.

Here, too, the beginnings are shrouded in legend; we have annals of fabulous dynasties that reigned "before the Flood." But as time passed, these ancient Sumerian settlements grew into city-states with written records of their own—Eridu, Larsa, Lagash, Nippur, and Ur, to name a few. All were small cities, with populations of between twelve and thirty-six thousand. The distances between towns were short: it was fifteen miles from Ur to Eridu, fifty miles between Ur and Erech, and Kish was just along the river from Babylon. Yet in spite of this compactness, Sumer never achieved a stable union as Egypt did; city-state fought city-state, and now and then one or another local king would bring the area under his rule. Nonetheless, the cities thrived, each under the protection of its ziggurat and god.

"As the waters of the Tigris and Euphrates flowed from the mountain to the plain, bringing nourishment for the crops, so the commands of the gods came from the heavens to the place of worship that linked heaven and earth." In the Sumerian belief, each city belonged to its god, and the king ruled or made war as the god's agent. The temple was the administrative and economic center, for which everyone worked. In its magazine were stored the surpluses of grain, oil, cloth, and precious objects, under an elaborate system of recording; and the high priest or *ensi* directed the bustling life of the community.

So, approaching any city of Sumer, you would see first across the flat expanse a high ziggurat surrounded by a thick wall. Many houses clustered about it. Then as you traveled towards town—on a busy highway between the irrigated fields with their wattled huts—you could mark sailboats threading along the canals and files of loaded donkeys heading up the valley, carrying Sumerian merchandise or bringing goods needed from faraway lands (metals and timber and stone were all lacking on that alluvial plain).

Now at last, entering the city by a guarded gate, you would wind your way down dirty crooked streets between low flat-topped mud-brick buildings. Through open doorways you would glimpse artisans at work, and you would pass shaded stands that held vegetables, copper pans, carpets, beads, pottery, even amulets from India. Finally, reaching the inner wall, you would show your credentials to a captain at the gate, and if they were satisfactory you would be permitted to enter. You were now in a park where palm trees sheltered you from the sun's heat. Here were the temples and palaces from which the priest-king governed the state. Here he lived with his court, his guards, scribes, priests, officials, artisans, and servants—while high on the shrine that topped the ziggurat sat the image of the god before his altar, the nominal center of all this enterprise.

Outside the city were the estates of the priest-kings and the vast lands of the temples, where peasants toiled under priestly overseers. They sowed and reaped, tended the beasts, watered the crops of barley and wheat in the blazing Sumerian sun—receiving in return their tools and seed, their rations of food and cloth. Some farmers did have their own holdings. But regimentation was necessary for the never-ending tasks of digging and clearing canals and building and repairing dikes. And inevitably there were oppressive abuses. The burden of Sumer's temple-system fell heaviest on the peasant who spent his days in the hot fields and his nights in a hut of wattled mud. Yet it also provided him compensations. Officially he belonged to the "household" of a deity. For several days each month and for a week and more at New Year's, he took part in the great religious Festivals in town—emotional rituals concerned with phases of the moon or the annual triumph of the generative forces of the earth. Even his hard toil was his way of serving the god whose protection he sought so anxiously. For beyond the fertile reclaimed Delta still lay a jungle land where elephants fed and swayed, lions roared, and snakes wound their certain way through trampled grass.

And inside the city, yet another new class served the ruling god: the specialized craftsmen. Bound together in guilds under the temple organization, these artisans worked in copper, tin, leather, wood, gold, silver, and semi-precious stones. They made metal tools and utensils, and pottery, for which they used the potter's wheel. They also wove gaily colored woolen cloth, made wagons, chariots, and plows, wrought superbly designed rings, earrings, beads, chains, pins, crowns, and helmets in gold, and mixed perfumes and cosmetics. The Sumerian sculpture which remains is crude; the architecture, as recovered by archaeologists from the dusty earth, is heavy-handed. But great delicacy marks one of their arts, a lesser art if you think in terms of size—the cutting of seals. The craft began, as far as we know, in Sumer. The seals were carved on cylinders of stone or metal, about an inch and a half long. These were rolled across wet clay and the impressions marked the signatures. Carved in high relief on these cylinders are gods, men, animals, trees, and the owner's name. Considering the tools of stone and copper the artist had, the results are amazing. The carvings are beautiful, both in design and workmanship.

Sumer was, indeed, a nation of craftsmen. Her story of the Great Flood, as told in the Babylonian Gilgamish epic, has a major difference from the Biblical one: On *his* ark, Uta-Napisthim took not only pairs of animals but also a shipload of treasures and artisans! And the skillful Sumerians made lasting contributions to mankind, both in the arts of peace and in the arts of war that developed from the struggle between their cities. Their city-states gave us notions of ordered government, formal laws regulating human behavior, and systematic ways of doing business. Their builders invented the arch and vault, devices that were to reach their glory and full usefulness in Rome. They were the first to use the military phalanx in battle; and more than two thousand years later Alexander would use phalanxes like these to conquer most of the known world. And they were probably the first people to use wheels, though the honor for the actual invention may belong to the adjoining Elamites.

Neighbor to Sumer, in the high hills north of the Persian Gulf, was the ancient kingdom of Elam. Its capital, Susa, was one of the most famous cities of the ancient world; today it is called Shushan. We can only guess who the Elamites were and where they came from, but archaeologists have found evidence that their culture dates back to before 3000 B. C. Theirs was a civilization of copper weapons and tools, of remarkable pottery which was made on a wheel, of hieroglyphic writing and carved seals, of idols. It was also a culture of jewels, cosmetics, mirrors, and containers to hold perfumes—for these last appear with the very earliest people. The Elamites probably invented the wheel, though the Sumerians used it. They grew grain, wheat, and barley; they raised domesticated animals, cattle, asses, goats, and sheep.

Of their history we know only that they warred with the nations of the adjoining valley, Sumer, Akkad, and Babylon. Sometimes they crossed the Tigris and Euphrates to return defeated and empty-handed, or again they came back with slaves and the loot of war. Susa was conquered at last by the ruthless Assyrians, whose warrior-king Ashurbanipal captured and ravaged her. But Darius the Great later restored her, and she became one of the capitals of his mighty Persian Empire.

Thus, through most of its history, the mountains of Elam kept that small kingdom secure, even while it took part in the wars that raged incessantly across the neighboring plain—the fabled Land Between the Two Rivers, where Western civilization began.

ZIGGURAT AT UR

The ziggurat—the hill of heaven, the mountain of God! Raised by Ur-Nammu and his son Shulgi of the Third Dynasty of Ur (2079-1960 B. C.) on the ruins of an earlier ziggurat, its great base stood for fifteen hundred years. The last king to repair the ancient temple was Nebuchadnezzar of Babylon.

II. Pyramids and Ziggurats

3000-2000 B. C.

Two gigantic shapes stand as symbols of the next thousand years: the Great Pyramid at Giza in Egypt; and the ruined brick levels of great ziggurats at Babylon and Ur, one of which, archaeologists believe, was the legendary Tower of Babel.

When the Great Pyramid was built by the Pharaoh Khufu, two million, three hundred thousand blocks of stone, each weighing two and a half tons, were dragged up ramps until they covered thirteen acres and reached a height of four hundred and eighty-one feet. Over this, an absolutely smooth outer facing of pure white limestone reflected the desert sun—truly a dazzling spectacle and one of the engineering marvels of ancient times. Those gigantic casing blocks were fitted with a joint no wider than a fiftieth of an inch! True, this splendid monument was raised by forced human labor: the conscripted peasants of Egypt, toiling and sweating in shifts of a hundred thousand during the spring floods of twenty years, not to mention the thousands more who worked in the quarries. Yet it had a profound meaning for the Egyptians. This pyramid-tomb was a fit eternal dwelling for their divine Pharaoh; it would protect his remains forever, assist his immortality, insure his continuing magical work for the Two Lands. Centuries afterward, to be sure, the burial-chamber was defiled by robbers, the gold and jewels of Khufu were stolen, and his mummy was thrown on the floor. But the Great Pyramid still stands in drifting sands, a wonder of the world and an enduring symbol of a brilliant age.

But memories of disaster surround the ruined ziggurats at Babylon and Ur—of the former only a huge hole is left. Archæologists believe that these gigantic terraced temples with their imposing causeways were the prototype of the fabulous Biblical tower raised by Noah's descendants on the Plain of Shinar in an effort to reach heaven, but abandoned when the builders found themselves speaking different languages. As a symbol, either will do. Both Sumerian buildings were interrupted or destroyed by wars. And ancient Sumer herself became the Empire of Sumer-Akkad, a kingdom of different tongues, repeatedly conquered and finally absorbed by aliens.

Yet both of these symbols need enlivening with a human figure. For the Pyramid Age was actually the flowering of early Egypt—an era of peace and lasting scientific and artistic progress. Probably the real genius of that age was Imhotep, architect, physician, statesman, a man of such vast talents and renown that Egyptians of later centuries worshiped him as a god. And his period (the Third Dynasty) began with a characteristic achievement: the improvement of the early "official" calendar. It had twelve months of thirty days each plus a final holiday-period of five more, making 365 days—or the average time between spring floods; and now it was pegged to a celestial phenomenon, the dawn each year when the Dog Star rose on the eastern horizon at Memphis. From this calendar of Imhotep's time derives the one we use today!

And though the Tower of Babel typifies destruction, it also stands for ambitious creation in Mesopotamia. There, too, the outstanding personality of the time, the conqueror Sargon the Great, lived on in popular folklore. And rightly so. His conquests were to obtain raw material for industry—wood and copper and silver; he promoted trade, communications, a "universal" language; and he established a wider rule of law and order. Indeed, Sargon's was the first model of many later empires that would help to spread civilization around the Mediterranean!

EGYPT IN THE PYRAMID AGE

The time is 2600 B. C., and the Old Kingdom is at its height. In her carrying chair sits Queen Hetep-Heres, mother of Khufu, first Pharoah of the Fourth Dynasty and builder of the Great Pyramid of Giza. Borne by slaves and attended by fan-bearers, she goes to an audience with her son. She wears a white robe and a fashionable wig of the period, bound by a tiara of gold. Around her slim neck is a circlet of carnelian, turquoise, and golden beads, and in one hand she carries a blossom of the sacred lotus. On the back of her chair, written in hieroglyphics, are the words: "Mother of the King of Upper and Lower Egypt, Follower of Horus, Guide of the Ruler. Favorite Lady."

THE PYRAMID AGE

Egypt's pyramids were the most spectacular achievements of a millennium of peace and prosperity. From the time of Menes, 3100 B. C., till the end of the Pyramid Age, 2180 B. C., the country had few wars. For those thousand years, a busy, hard-working, intelligent people irrigated its fields, worshiped its gods, erected beautiful buildings, created great art, and made amazing inventions in engineering and other sciences. Today the mighty monuments of that age can be seen near Memphis: pyramids, tombs, and shrines, stretching along the desert's edge for sixty miles.

The earliest or so-called Step Pyramid was built around 2700 B. C. for the Pharaoh Zoser, founder of the Third Dynasty, by Imhotep himself. This great vizier's edifice—it had forty-two steps and rose to a height of 190 feet like a giant staircase ascending toward heaven—was a daring innovation. Though using methods adapted from brickwork, Imhotep laid the basis for large-scale stone masonry: his is the oldest free-standing stone structure known. Temples of limestone were built beside it, and here fluted columns were first used.

A hundred years after Zoser's death the Pharaoh Khufu of the Fourth Dynasty sought to live forever by erecting as his tomb the Great Pyramid of Giza. For five hundred years after that, pyramid after pyramid was built, each for a different king, and each surrounded by mastaba tombs. Massive roofed oblongs of masonry with walls slanting at a seventy-five-degree angle, the mastabas held chapels served by an endowed priesthood. Far below, reached through a shaft in the native rock resealed with sand or gravel, was the burial chamber where lay the mummified body, ears and mouth open to harken and speak in the hereafter, resting on its left side in a casket of Lebanon cedar encased in a granite or limestone sarcophagus. These were the tombs of members of the royal family and the great men who served them, clustered about the pyramids, making in death a pattern of a Pharaoh's court. Side by side with this monumental architecture, sculpture flourished. Enormous images of gods and Pharaohs were carved in wood and stone. The Great Sphinx, the largest portrait ever sculptured, was probably the likeness of the Pharaoh Khafre, third ruler of the Fourth Dynasty.

But another art is more interesting to us. In the tomb chapels with

EGYPTIAN CATTLE

All the land in Egypt belonged theoretically to the Pharaoh. Once a
year an account of profit or loss had to be sent to the royal tax-gath-
erers, along with the tax due (paid in kind). Here in his pavilion a
noble named Thut sits with his scribes, who are making up his annual
record for the officials, and counts his cattle as they are slowly driven
by. It has been a fat year, with plentiful crops; the god-Pharaoh has
kept the irrigation system in repair; and there is peace in the land.
With his taxes and rents paid, his cattle healthy, and his bins over-
flowing with grain, the nobleman will go to the temple and place
rich gifts on the altar of Isis, giving thanks to the earth goddess and
looking forward hopefully to another prosperous year.

their picture-biographies of the deceased, and in the great murals that adorned temples and palaces, the consummate illustrators of ancient Egypt depicted the entire life of their land and its heaven. The Old Kingdom seems to come alive from those modeled and painted walls.

Memphis was the capital and metropolis of Egypt during the Pyramid Age. There in great palaces and temples, surrounded by nobles and priests, the Pharaohs lived, worshiped, and ruled. Advised by wise men and attended by priests and scribes, they questioned the governors of the provinces, they received embassies, they heard petitions and directed the affairs of their kingdom.

For this was the center of an ordered economy—in theory, the divine Pharaoh owned all the fertile land of Egypt and was in charge of all aspects of Egyptian life. Actually, every acre was taxed in kind, and so was all industry and trade. And a vast bureaucracy regulated the teeming, lengthy country, from Pharaoh's vizier and treasurer and agriculture minister, through a host of minor functionaries, clear down to the local governors or nomarchs and their staffs. So in Memphis huge buildings of brick housed the royal warehouses and granaries and offices, where officials, clerks, and scribes worked at keeping records and accounts, while tax collectors made reports of taxes received and due. The rest of the city consisted of low buildings of sun-dried brick, the houses and shops of the common people.

Along the busy streets and in the market-places went donkeys laden with produce from the great river estates. Here housewives traded for food, women carried jars of oil on their heads, servants bore noblewomen in carrying chairs, and priests hurried to temples. Here too a caravan from the desert brought gold and precious stones for the Pharaoh, palace guards loitered before the wineshops, and fat scribes sat cross-legged in doorways, writing letters for their clients. Dogs, cats, and children played in the sun, and merchants cried their wares or haggled with buyers. All trade was carried on by barter, for money was unknown. In buildings or under porches, skilled artisans made jewelry, glass, pottery, and furniture, or fashioned objects of linen and paper, or shaped statues.

Both men and women wore simple clothes of linen; the wall paintings and the bas-reliefs show the style of dress, which was to change slightly from century to century. Everyone was bedecked with jewelry —from the stone necklaces of the poor to the magnificent ornaments of amethyst, carnelian, jasper, turquoise, and gold, worn by the rich. The well-to-do of both sexes affected heavy black wigs to protect their heads from the sun and to be in style, and ladies of wealth plaited their perfumed hair, filled it with artificial tresses, and trimmed the mass with gold circlets. They had beauty experts and hairdressers, and used oils, perfumes, rouge, and green eye-shadow; and this was more than four thousand years ago!

In fact, throughout the history of Egypt women had social rights unusual in ancient times. Descent was frequently through the female line. On marriage a woman retained her own property; after children were born, she was legal "mistress of the house" even if it was originally the man's; and if she was widowed she became head of the family. She could be the suitor in love, and she sometimes did the proposing.

City life had its gay side, too. Men and women, adorned with garlands of leaves and flowers, attended fashionable banquets. Musicians, dancers, and acrobats amused them, while magicians told their fortunes and performed tricks. At home, games were played with checkers and dice. The rich had pleasure boats on the Nile, and lotus pools and shaded gardens were set along the palm-edged river bank.

Between the towns and cities stretched the farmlands, mostly great tracts belonging to Pharaoh himself or granted by him to temples and nobles. Here and there were poor plots tilled by small landowners. But the rich land was in vast, flourishing estates cultivated by serfs, and many of these were self-suffcent units. They employed not only farmers but scribes, potters, carpenters, smiths, masons, boatmen, and also women to do the cooking, spinning, and weaving.

Early in the morning the noble owner, with his overseer, inspected

PLOWING

Above are two Egyptians with their ox-drawn plow, turning the fertile black acres of the Pharaoh, on the west bank of the Nile. In the distance rise two of those extraordinary tombs, the Pyramids, that edge the desert for sixty miles south of Memphis. Across the sky fly the sacred ibis, messengers of Thoth, the Egyptian god of wisdom.

his crops and irrigation systems and saw that his serfs were hard at work, plowing, seeding, harvesting, or tending the herds. He spent the hot hours of the day in the ease and beauty of his house and gardens, surrounded by his family. Looking across his lush fields to the sandstone cliffs beyond the river, and seeing an ever-cloudless sky above the flooded Nile, he must have given thanks to Osiris for the beautiful land of green, gold, and blue, and for peace and plenty.

In the cool of the evening that nobleman might walk with his wife under the palm trees at the river's edge, watching the boats pass up and down the Nile; or he might gaze in awe and admiration at the distant temples and tombs. For his sport he trapped waterfowl in the marshes, and sometimes he went beyond the cataracts of the Nile to spear hippopotamuses, or even into Nubia to hunt lions.

Of course, this life of elegance rested on the forced labor of the peasants—not only in the fields of their noble masters, but on lavish public works during the flood season. It was the peasants who sweated under the hot sun, irrigating the land with the waters of the Nile, making the bricks, building the temples and the royal tombs. Yet they were not grim toilers. Their hard existence kept some moments of gaiety: harvesters worked to flute music, there was occasionally fresh shade and clear water, and evening brought a draft of beer and the merry games of children. Certainly there was an ideal of a harmonious relation between Pharaoh, officials, and people; and the famous Vizier Ptahhotep did urge integrity in his "Proverbs." But in practice, rulers were forever having to admonish and to mete out punishment to their unjust and oppressive agents. Peasants were virtually chattels, just above beasts of burden. The typical field-hand was slender and not fully fed; if his work was unsatisfactory he could be beaten with rods, and he might be taken away from home to serve in a state labor gang. Most revealing of all, during this period the masses had no share in the afterlife.

So it is not surprising that in the latter centuries of the Old Kingdom the absolutism of the Memphite Pharaohs collapsed into feudalism. It was a slow crumbling. The exaggerated splendor of pyramids and temples had strained the resources of the land; their upkeep, by tax-exempt endowments, impoverished the royal treasury. Meantime, the nomarchs of the provinces grew in arrogance and power and acquired hereditary status, becoming virtual landed rulers with only a doubtful loyalty to the king. The Fifth Dynasty was overthrown, though the convulsion was brief. For a while the able Pharaoh Pepi I, third of the Sixth Dynasty, kept order, controlled the nobles, chose strong and able administrators; his armies invaded Nubia, his fleets raided the Asian coast as far as Phoenicia, his son and successor Merenre built canals and explored the Sudan. But under his grandson Pepi II, whose ninety-year reign was the longest in history, the deterioration went on. On his death the country broke into small, disputing states. No longer

EGYPTIAN RIVER BOAT

An Egyptian river boat with its double mast is sailing up the Nile from
Memphis to Elephantine. On the return voyage, facing the constant
north wind, the sail will be unfurled, the mast unstepped; the strong
arms of Nubian oarsmen will furnish the power. In exchange for a
cargo of goods from the Delta, this boat will bring back to Memphis
wealth from Africa—gold, ivory, ebony, skins, feathers, certainly some
monkeys, and perhaps a pygmy for the court of Pharaoh Pepi of the
Sixth Dynasty.

could the Pharaohs curb the hereditary nobles, and anarchy prevailed
throughout Egypt. Revolutions covered the land. Mobs pillaged
the towns; the irrigation systems were wrecked; destruction was
rampant.

Now the nomarchs or governors ruled; this was the Feudal Age.
The power of the Pharaohs was in eclipse. For almost three hundred
and fifteen years Heracleopolis was the capital. Memphis was no longer
the place of the Great House.

Yet this dark turmoil brought forth new moral values. The Egyptians began to believe that their gods did more than rule the Nile and

dispense material favors. Osiris and the others were seen as arbiters of right and wrong, dispensers of justice and mercy—and surely kindness and good will would count when a man's soul came to be weighed against a feather!

And ultimately there was a restoration. A powerful family of nobles, in the obscure town of Thebes some four hundred miles south of the Delta's mouth, gradually extended their rule by force and guile all the way to the First Cataract. Their Theban god, Amon, became the national Amon-Ra. Theirs was the Eleventh Dynasty, the first of the Thebans: two Intefs, then five Mentuhoteps. The last Mentuhotep was Pharaoh of Upper and Lower Egypt, wearer of the double crown, lord of the whole land, for fifty years. But the glory of the Old Kingdom was gone.

SUMER-AKKAD

During the peace of Egypt's Pyramid Age, constant wars and invasions were bringing new masters to the fertile fields of Mesopotamia.

First of these new rulers were the Akkadians, a tribe of Semites who had entered the Plain of Shinar from the west and infiltrated into the region around modern Baghdad. Perhaps because Sumer was weakened by continual civil war, they were able to seize the towns of Kish and Opis.

Next they turned southward, but found their archers no match for Sumerian soldiers and phalanxes. Eventually, however, these virile northerners adopted the culture and weapons and strategy of the Sumerians, and were able to conquer and rule the whole region. Their influence was to be a lasting one—thenceforth the land would have two tongues, the old Sumerian and the new Semitic—and they swept into power under the leadership of the area's first mighty monarch.

Sargon the Great was a man with no family. An abandoned baby found floating on the Euphrates in a rush basket, as Moses was found

CARAVAN

Here you see a Sumerian-Akkadian caravan crossing the plain between
the Two Rivers. Slaves and the patient donkey are the beasts of burden
—two thousand years will pass before camels will be used.

on the Nile, he was taken home and raised by a laborer. Later, he became a royal page and then cup-bearer to Ur-Ilbaba, second king of the
Fourth Dynasty of Kish. His career began when he led a successful
palace revolution and seated himself on the throne of Kish, to become
a great king and a god in about 2350 B. C. Then he left Kish and built
his capital city of Agade fifty miles above Babylon on the Euphrates.
Thence he marched northwest up the valley with his army, subduing
city after city. His own record states that he "conquered as far as the
cedar forests and the silver mountains," that is, Lebanon and the mountains of Cilicia. On another expedition he reached Cappadocia in Asia
Minor, slaying thousands on the way. Having the north (or Akkad
proper) in hand, Sargon turned south toward his rival Lugal-Zaggisi,

FALL

the head of a Sumerian empire that reached from the Persian Gulf to the Mediterranean. Now Sargon invaded Sumer, defeated the Sumerian army, and carried the captive king to Nippur. Ur and Umma followed, and soon Sargon was master of the whole land, lord of Sumer and Akkad. So great was his fame that sixteen hundred years later one of the powerful kings of Assyria took his name, and Sargon the Great is remembered throughout Mesopotamia to this day.

Yet Sargon's dynasty was to fall before nomadic invaders. His grandson, Naram-Sin, the "favorite" of the moon-god, extended the empire until it reached north to Armenia and west to the Mediterranean coast. Near Susa he set up a stone slab, or stele, which depicts him slaughtering a tribe of nomads. But during the reign of the last Sargonian monarch, the Guti nomads from the Zagros mountains, north of the Tigris, invaded and conquered the land that Sargon the Great had won. After violating the altars and despoiling the gods, they established a dynasty of their own that lasted a hundred and twenty-five years. The

AKKADIAN MERCHANTS

Two Akkadian merchants are watching their Sumerian clerk while he
writes a letter on a clay tablet. Their merchandise, in large bales and
carefully marked, will be shipped by boat on the navigable canals.
(In the graves at Ur were found small models of river boats, very like
those that sail on the Euphrates today. Changes are slow in the East.)

Guti rulers came and went, twenty in all, with an average reign of only
six years. Under them, Gudea, Sumerian king of Lagash, was a great
builder of temples and patron of the arts. Archaeologists have found
eighteen portrait statues of him, carved in diorite: a squarish massive

figure with painted eyes and nails, sitting or standing stiffly, hands firmly folded and feet planted together, and sometimes a plan on his lap. But these statues are not in a class with the exquisite seal-carvings —the Sumerian craftsmen were not quite at home in monumental stone.

The rule of the nomads ended when a Guti monarch was abandoned in battle by his troops and made a prisoner of Utu-Khegal of Erech. But the new kingdom was short-lived. It ended when Utu-Khegal made the mistake of appointing as *patesi* of Ur a man of more decision than loyalty.

This Ur-Nammu promptly revolted and founded the lavish dynasty of Ur. First he captured Erech and the king who had appointed him, then he marched on with his army and made himself master of the land. Thenceforth he ruled as the mighty man, King of Ur, King of Sumer and Akkad. Ur remained his capital, and the main divinity there was the moon-god Nannar. A conqueror's first duty was to honor his patron deity and make it head god in all the conquered cities. So Ur-Nammu began the building of a great ziggurat to the moon-god at Ur. He also raised temples to Nannar in Lagash, Eridu, and Umma. In fact, he became a great builder, constructing roads and clearing the canals of silt. And, after ruling eighteen years, he died in peace.

His son, Shulgi, followed him as a god-king. He organized his father's conquests and added a few of his own. Then, remembering his duty, he finished the great ziggurat at Ur, which his father had started. The bricks all bore his name and seal, for throughout the long history of Mesopotamia bricks used by a king's builder were inscribed with the royal name. Shulgi reigned in peace and prosperity for forty-seven years. His son succeeded him as "King of Ur, King of the Four Quarters of the Earth," and was also deified.

But the dynasty was weakening. One ruler built a wall in the north, instead of taking offensive action against the threat of invasion. And finally the invaders came from both sides. From the west the Amorites of Babylon overran and conquered Akkad. From the east the Elamites

SUMERIAN KING AND GOD

Ur-Nammu, King of Ur, stands with bowed head before Nannar, the
Moon God, while an attendant kneels in awe. The divinity holds in his
hand a measuring rod and the coiled rope of the architect, indicating
that he expects the monarch to erect a great temple in his honor.
Needless to say, a ziggurat will be built.

crossed the Tigris and captured Ur. They demolished the city, robbed
its graves, loaded its wealth onto their wagons, and led its king back
to Susa in chains. Behind them they left the devastated "Hill of
Heaven," the ziggurat to the moon-god of Ur. Was that the Tower of
Babel—or was it the larger and more ancient ziggurat left unfinished
in the conquests of Babylon? Either way, the fall of Ur about 1950 B. C.
marked the end of the empire of Sumer-Akkad.

"THERE IS AN ISLE CALLED CRETE"

But the fall of power need not mean the death of a civilization. The great accomplishments of Sumer—cuneiform writing, the wheel, splendid crafts, the arch and vault, military tactics—were passed on by her successive conquerors. The Semitic Akkadians ceased to rule, but for hundreds of years their language remained the international means of communication in Western Asia. And during her centuries of peace and plenty, Egypt too had been sharing a brilliant culture with many neighbors. The trading ships of the Pharaohs sailed to the islands of the Aegean and the coast of Asia Minor, and down the Red Sea and into the Indian Ocean. They brought cedar and cypress from Lebanon

EGYPTIAN CARGO SHIP

Sailing down the Phoenician coast, this Egyptian ship is returning from Tyre with a valuable load of cedar cut in the forests of Lebanon. Since Egypt had practically no wood of her own, the Egyptians built most of their graceful furniture with this cedar. An Egyptian of high rank was always buried in a coffin of Lebanon cedar wood.

CARAVANSARY

It is late afternoon, and a caravan bound from Sumer to Egypt has stopped at this Syrian caravansary to spend the night. The donkeys are being relieved of their burdens and will soon be fed. Men sit around a fire and eat hunks of lamb roasted on skewers (the same dish, known as shish-kebab, is still prepared in the Near East). After supper, the one gate to the courtyard will be locked and barred, and everyone will go to sleep early. For the caravan must be off at dawn, to reach the next town before the midday heat, so the traders can rest and eat there and do some business.

and Syria, and copper from Cyprus and the Sinai peninsula. From Nubia in the south caravans of donkeys brought strange tropical luxuries—ebony, ivory, ostrich feathers, and gold. And ever since very early times other caravans had made their way from Egypt across a wilderness of sand and stone to trade for the treasures of Sumer-Akkad. All the caravans and ships were heavily guarded, for robbers and pirates infested the deserts and seas; and everywhere they brought or left the products of Egyptian arts and skills and sciences. One particular trading center, much influenced by Egypt in this period, was later to develop a beautiful and graceful culture of its own.

"There is an isle called Crete in wine-dark seas, a fair rich land begirt with water, and therein are many men past counting and ninety cities." Thus wrote Homer, the Greek poet. But by the fifth century B. C. classical Greece had forgotten all about Crete. And by modern times the Cretans or Minoans had become a mere legend. Only the myths of Theseus and the Minotaur and the flight of Icarus were remembered.

Then, after three thousand years of oblivion, Minoan culture was rediscovered by an English archaeologist. Sir Arthur Evans was fascinated by some inscribed amulets he had bought in Athens, and traced them to Crete. There in 1900, after long negotiations, he purchased what he thought was the site of Knossos, the ancient capital. Within a few weeks his diggers had uncovered the burned ruins of the great Minoan city and with it a civilization long believed to have been a myth. It was one of the great finds of all time. Sir Arthur had unearthed an entire culture: the supposed labyrinth of the Minotaur, or an intricate foundation plan that resembled it; the stone temples and decorated palaces of Minos; the sun-dried brick houses of traders, artisans, and workers, and their goods and tools. Here, too, was a record of the teeming life of burned Knossos, on clay tablets hardened and preserved by fire—the writing was the same as on the original amulets.

For decades the Minoan tablets remained unread. But in 1953 a brilliant young English scholar found the key to their decipherment: some are in archaic Greek, and others, surprisingly, in ancient Akkadian! Translation is now going forward, and soon we may learn more about the political life of the Cretans, their wars, laws, and literature, their kings and queens. Perhaps, too, we may learn the basis of the story of Minos and his labyrinth and sacred bull, and exactly where the Minoans came from. But, for the time being, the ruins and the delightfully frescoed walls tell us the story of the sea kingdom of Crete.

On a beautiful island in the Mediterranean Sea a remarkable civilization began about 3000 B. C.—when migrants from Anatolia brought farming, pottery-making, and building skills to a people just emerging from the Stone Age. These Cretans belonged to the "Mediterranean" race that was found all over the Levant and North Africa in those days; their paintings show them as short, slender, dark-haired. Their island was strategically situated as a shipping center, bound to receive and spread influences: sixty miles to the north was Greece, and three hundred and forty miles southeast was the mouth of the River Nile. And on this small island, only a hundred and sixty miles long and thirty-five miles at the widest, a highly original culture was to develop during more than fifteen hundred years.

During that long period Crete was protected by her fleet and safe from any serious invasion. But there seem to have been internal troubles aplenty. Ruins upon ruins show us how her cities—destroyed by earthquakes, revolutions, or civil wars—rose again and again, each time greater than before. With every rebuilding, the life and art of Crete became finer, until it reached a peak of unique beauty and elegance. But in this first or Early Minoan period, Crete was still *receiving* culture: her art was strongly Egyptian in style, her crafts inferior to those of Sumer-Akkad. Her own flowering was yet to come. For the progress of civilization around the Mediterranean was a slow, irregular stream, with great centers flourishing and dying while others were still being born.

KING HAMMURABI

Here the great King of Babylon questions two of his tax-collectors, who have apparently been remiss. Either they have failed to collect monies due the king, or they have collected and failed to deliver. One official kneels as a suppliant; the other doubtfully awaits the royal decision. On each side of Hammurabi stands a scribe to record the verdict, and a guard waits to take the officials to their death, if they are found guilty.

III.   The Scene Widens: Babylonia, Hatti, Egypt, Crete

2000-1580 B. C.

During the next five centuries, erstwhile barbarians—with bronze weapons and horses—overran the eastern Mediterranean. Hitherto, the wealthy lands on the Nile and Euphrates had sent war and trade expeditions to the vast primitive areas beyond. Now these wild invaders poured into the spreading stream of civilization. And from the upheavals of the era, *four* great centers emerged: a revived Babylonia; ancient Egypt, resplendent once more; the new Empire of Hatti; and the sea-kingdom of Crete.

Horses came into Mesopotamia by 2000 B. C., around the time that semibarbarous Amorites, a Semitic tribe from Syria, took over the decrepit Empire of Sumer-Akkad. Their vigorous rule was marked by the rise of Babylon. And Babylon attained its first period of magnificence under the greatest king of the Amorite dynasty: the famous empire-builder, Hammurabi.

Somewhat later the tactical use of horses in war led to the appearance of a new "third force" in the Mediterranean, the Empire of Hatti. When the Hittites had fought their way into Asia Minor, a few centuries before, they were a barbaric people, a tribe of Indo-Europeans from somewhere north of the Black Sea. Once settled, they began to learn the ways of civilization from their neighbors, Babylonian traders, Assyrians, and especially the horse-breeding Hurrians of Mitanni. Having acquired swift steeds, the Hittites proceeded to yoke them to the latest terrible engine of war—they perfected the light battle-chariot with open six-spoked wheels (a far cry from the heavy solid-wheeled Sumerian cart drawn by asses). With their new mobile army they became in time the masters of all Asia Minor. The story of the great Hittite Federation, forgotten and lost for centuries, is one of the exciting discoveries of modern archaeology.

Farthest away from the threat of invasions lay the ancient land of Egypt. Under her Middle Kingdom she enjoyed a brilliant and broadened revival from the darkness of her Feudal Age—gigantic engineering works now had a social usefulness. But finally she fell, conquered by the semi-barbarian Hyksos or "shepherd kings," an obscure Semitic and Hurrian people with chariots and horses.

Still the area of civilization was widening, and more centers meant more commerce. It is no accident that this period saw the rise of the world's first maritime power: the Minoan island of Crete, with its palaces, craftsmen, and fleet of ships plying the "wine-dark seas."

BABYLONIA UNDER HAMMURABI

It was from Babylon, a small town where they settled on the Euphrates River, that the Syrian Amorites began their conquest of Mesopotamia. Sumer-Akkad, already at war with Elam, faced them hopelessly. Yet constant fighting consumed the reigns of the first five Amorite kings; even when the sixth of the line, the great Hammurabi, ascended the throne, it took him thirty years to defeat the Elamites. But one by one the ancient cities were taken, the eastern invaders were finally driven back to their mountains, and the Plain of Shinar became the Plain of Babylon—the Empire of Babylonia.

Babylonia's culture was Sumerian. All the inventions and literature and religion of ancient Sumer became hers. Her language, at least that of her merchants and workers, was the Semitic Akkadian tongue, though priests and scholars used classic Sumerian. But her codified law and order, though based on the mass of previous laws, have been celebrated from ancient to modern times as the work of the lawgiver Hammurabi.

Hammurabi lived twelve years after his victories. He devoted his time of peace to establishing a rule of order throughout his kingdom and forming a standing army to protect that order. From the clay tablets of Babylon we have a complete picture of his reign, and one find in particular tells us of his most celebrated achievement.

This monarch had the ancient laws of Sumer collected and codified into what is known as the Code of Hammurabi. He had these laws inscribed on an eight-foot diorite shaft and placed in the temple of the Babylonian "great god" Marduk. Above the text on the shaft was a relief showing Hammurabi receiving the laws from the high god himself, so that all the worshipers might behold their source and those who could might read them. The stone itself was discovered in Susa and is now in the Louvre Museum in Paris.

To us the laws seem very harsh. They called for justice for the weak and poor, but their main theme was "an eye for an eye." They regulated every business and profession, prescribed the penalty for every offense. Heavy fines were imposed for striking a man; amputations, torture, and death were to be exacted for crimes of violence or theft. These, so far as we know, were the first written laws designed for a universal rather than a local application—to "establish justice in Sumer and Akkad."

Under the law and order of Hammurabi's reign, the Babylonians grew rich, their flocks and herds increased. Now the guarded donkey caravans of Babylon, loaded with bales of goods safely roped and sealed, traded along the two rivers. These caravans traveled into the mountains of Asia Minor, to the shores of the Mediterranean Sea, or down the canal Hammurabi had built from Kish to the Persian Gulf. Trade was in the hands of the rich merchants and richer priests, and all was regulated by the laws of Hammurabi.

Learning flourished too, in the many temples. Stealing or adopting gods was a common practice, so by this time there was a merry-go-round of gods in Babylon. The Babylonians kept their great god Marduk as high god, with Ishtar, goddess of love, in second place. But they appropriated the deities of Sumer and Sumer-Akkad, and built shrines and established priesthoods for them also. And the Babylonian priests became the astronomers of the ancient world.

Astronomy and astrology were developed as part of their religion with its basic fatalism. Planets and fixed stars, as visible forms of gods, ruled human destinies. From the position of the stars the priests claimed to read a man's future. As they fussed with portents and signs to plan horoscopes, these priests scanned the heavens, noting the position of moon, stars, and planets. And gradually they were able to measure time and celestial movements with this knowledge.

In addition, schools existed in Babylon. Students had clay tablets of questions and answers, as well as tablets of arithmetic—a study useful to future traders. And tales of gods and heroes were inscribed on their reading tablets. In an inner court, open to the sky, the pupils marked their lessons with a stylus on soft clay; at recess they played at war.

Such was Babylon as we read about it on thousands of clay tablets. Some of them record the business of a great commercial empire: bills, receipts, lists, costs, agreements, collections, law-suits, and credit and debit charges. Others disclose the king's doings, his orders, laws, taxes, charges and commands sent by messengers to the governors and tax-collectors of the provinces. Again we can trace on these tablets the progress of the Babylonians in mathematics and science. Besides all this, we find prayers, hymns, and poems, the tales of the Flood and the Garden of Eden, the epic of the great hero Gilgamesh, and the stories of gods such as Naal, Shamash, Tammuz, and a hundred others.

But beyond the tablets of clay, nothing remains of Hammurabi's city of bricks. Little of Babylon's art survives, almost none from this period. What sculpture we have is inferior to the work of Sumerians and Akkadians, not even in a class with that of the Egyptians. These Babylonians were not artists but clever tradesmen and learned priests. And after the death of the great Hammurabi the decline of their empire followed quickly. The half-civilized Kassites began entering the Plain of Babylon, and eventually they conquered it.

Meanwhile, farther to the north, revolt was stirring among the subject Assyrians. Around 2500 B. C. this tribe of Semitic nomads had left the desert and settled on the Tigris, two hundred miles above Babylon. Their town of Ashur was named after their head god, and it became their capital. For a long time they were ruled by *patesis* appointed by the Babylonian kings. These Assyrians grew rich, perhaps because their settlement was on the caravan route between the Persian Gulf and the silver mines of Cilicia. But they were on the invasion route too, and an unceasing war for survival toughened them. First the Hittites invaded their land, then the Babylonians held it. The Mitanni horsemen raided and robbed them for years and for a while kept them in vassalage. And they fought continuously against Cimmerian and Scythian nomads on their northern border. It was savage and brutal war, enslaving, mutilating, massacring, the same old story that had been going on in Mesopotamia since earliest times. But the Assyrians became the acknowledged masters of the ugly art. During the rule of the Kassites, they finally rebelled and declared their independence—one more step in the break-up of Hammurabi's law and order.

THE MYSTERY OF THE HITTITES

While Babylon rose and fell, the new Empire of the Hittites was coming into being farther west. How we know about these people is one of the most exciting adventures in archaeology.

For centuries strange ruins were a mystery throughout Syria and Asia Minor: ancient cities, cliffs covered with sculptures of gods and warriors, of lions and winged beasts, inscriptions in unreadable hieroglyphics, clay tablets marked with an unknown script. No one could tell who made them. The mystery had been heightened by the discovery in 1843, near the great bend of the Halys River, of the ruins of an immense metropolis protected by huge walls. Theory followed theory, but little credence was given to the British scholar A. H. Sayce, who pointed to Biblical evidence and attributed the ruins to the Hittites. Then in 1887 a great haul of cuneiform tablets was found at Tel-el-Amarna on the Nile, amid the ruins of the holy city of the Pharaoh Akhnaton. Many were official letters dealing with relations between the Egyptian and Hittite courts. The long-lost Empire of Hatti was again a historical reality!

More and more excavations followed, but it was another sixty years before the inscriptions could be read. In 1913 a Czech scholar, Friedrich Hrozny, announced that Hittite belonged to the Indo-European family of languages. Now the script spoke, and, with every tablet translated, men learned how the Hittites had lived and loved and died.

ROYAL HITTITES

A Hittite king and his buxom wife are drinking a libation to their
weather god or to good fortune. Behind each chair a maid with
switches keeps the ever-present flies from annoying them. The detail
is taken from Hittite sculpture.

But the strange hieroglyphics were still silent. Then, in 1947, Helmuth
T. Bossert found the long-sought "bilingual" on the Black Mountain of
Karatepe in the Taurus Range of southeastern Turkey (ancient Cilicia).
There it was, in Phoenician script and Hittite hieroglyphics, on some
reliefs of a petty king who had ruled twenty-six hundred years ago! At
last the deciphering could be completed and the rest of the story
filled in.

The history of the Hittites, as we now know it, begins with a curse
that failed to work. Some time after 1900 B. C., one Anittas, a local ruler,
attacked, captured, and burned the city of Hattusas, cursing the ruins
with an appeal to the chief Hittite divinity: "Whoever rebuilds Hattusas, may the weather god strike him!" But Hattusas was rebuilt and
became the capital of the kingdom of Hatti, believed to have been
founded by Labarnas, 1680-1650 B. C. This monarch — whose name

came to be a synonym for "king," just as Caesar's did later for "Roman emperor" — succeeded mainly by force in uniting the petty city-states under his rule and establishing the king's right to name his successor, under a new legal provision. But the dynasty was beset with family troubles. His son Hattusilis I safely ascended the throne and enlarged the southern boundary as far as Aleppo, only to return home ill and disinherit a heartless nephew. A grandson, Mursilis I, succeeded him and engaged in many military ventures, climaxed by a trip down the Euphrates to raid Babylon itself. He returned laden with loot, marching through the streets of Hattusas amid cheering crowds — and entered his palace to meet death at the hands of a brother-in-law in 1590 B. C. Nevertheless, during his reign, Mursilis changed the original loose association of cities into an empire that was to become in time the third great power of the Near East, the equal of Babylonia and Egypt.

But Hatti never created a culture of her own; she just took what she found. In art the Hittites were poor imitators. They made monolithic carvings of standard-looking gods, long clumsy processions of the usual priests and warriors, bas-reliefs of lions and bulls that were cult symbols throughout the region. Their architecture was plain and utilitarian. Neither temples nor palaces, but great defensive walls characterized their cities: Hattusas had a main wall with many towered gates, and a secondary wall twenty feet farther out. Yet this easy acceptance of other cultures was Hatti's administrative strength.

From their capital city of Hattusas — in northern Asia Minor, east of the modern Turkish capital of Ankara — the Hittites actually ruled over a federation of city-states scattered across Asia Minor and Syria. These cities were separated by many miles of mountainous country, connected only by caravan trails. Under Hittite rule they maintained their own languages and their own religions and were never consolidated into a homogeneous nation. From inscriptions we know that as many as eight different tongues were spoken in Hattusas: each meant a different subject tribe and another set of gods. Over all these divinities was the greatest god of the Hittites — the weather-god Tes-

HITTITE GATE

Every hundred feet the long wall encircling Hattusas, capital of the
Hittite Empire, was pierced with one of these double-towered gates.
Here the usual trading is going on. To the right are Hittite guards, who
checked on everyone entering or leaving the city. And through the
gate in the town you see a low serrated wall which could be reached
by tunnels in case of a siege.

hub, lord of winds and storms, lightning and thunder. But his was an
indulgent rule.

In the Hittite social order we see this same tendency. Theirs was a
feudal system, but it was not rigid; a common man might rise to the
caste of a noble, and there was no great difference between high and
low. And the Hittite laws far surpassed in humaneness the strict "eye
for an eye" punishments of Hammurabi. Listen to one: "If a man breaks
a freeman's leg or arm, he pays him twenty shekels of silver." Wrongs

STREET SCENE IN EGYPT

These two pages show the Nile riverfront in ancient Thebes during the Middle Kingdom. You see a busy port, crowded with venders, buyers, shopkeepers, workmen, sailors and traders from Asia and Africa. The sun-dried brick buildings are filled with the produce of the Nile Valley. In the background, men are loading a seagoing ship that will set sail in the morning, going down-river and out through the Delta, and then across the Mediterranean to Knossos in Crete.

were redressed not by a like wrong, but by restitution or compensation to the injured party — or reformation might even be asked of the offender! In their humane code — as in their constitutional monarchy and their federation of states — the Hittites were among the first to show administrative tolerance.

THE MIDDLE KINGDOM AND ITS FALL

Around the time the Hittites were entering history, Egypt was flourishing anew under the able despots of her Middle Kingdom.

Adding to the congestion of the street are the ubiquitous donkeys. One, ridden by a young boy, is watched by a spotted Egyptian dog with pointed ears. If you look carefully you will find a cat, considered by the Egyptians to be a sacred animal. In the Delta city of Bubastis, the cat achieved the dignity of a god and was worshiped as the "Goddess Bast."

Once again a real centralized government was established to hold the nomarchs in check. And for two centuries the great Twelfth Dynasty — four rulers called Amenemhet, three called Sesostris, not to mention the last, who was a queen — restored Egypt to much of her former splendor. Amenemhet I expanded his land, fortified his frontiers, rebuilt the irrigation system, and opened a canal connecting the Nile with the Red Sea. His successors extended their southern boundary to the Second Cataract and controlled the river valley for a thousand miles. The mines of Nubia poured gold into their coffers; copper came from the mines of Sinai and the island of Cyprus. Another canal now carried shipping past the First Cataract, and Egypt's fleet sailed the

Red Sea, traded with Punt, and went all the way along the coast of Phoenicia to the Aegean Sea. For the first time, under Sesostris III, a Pharaoh invaded Syria and returned with wealth and slaves.

All these feats of trade and conquest were topped by a spectacular engineering project. Sixty miles south of the Delta lay a great swamp, the Fayum, made by the flooding river waters. This swampy area the Pharaoh Amenemhet III divided in two by means of a retaining wall twenty-seven miles long. Half of the swamp now became a reservoir for use when the Nile was low; the other half was drained and yielded thousands of acres of land to be cultivated. At this period too the height and time of the annual Nile flood was first recorded on rocks at the Second Cataract; this information was then carried by messengers to the Delta, where the Pharaoh's officials estimated the size of the year's crop and the taxes due the king. Small wonder that after his death Amenemhet III was deified and worshiped as Prammares, god of the Fayum.

Nor was progress solely material. The fine arts reached new levels of beauty and delicacy, and this was the great age of Egyptian literature. Now there were moving poems, the joyous "Song of the Harper," the somber "Dispute of a Man with His Soul," and songs for the rich at their feasts and songs for the workers in their fields; sacred dramas and hymns for religious festivals, and treatises on embalming, geometry, medicine, history, and astronomy. Papyrus books recorded all the learning of Egypt. And scribes set down a real literature of entertainment: stories of magicians, the romantic yarn of the warrior Prince Sinuhe, and such popular folk tales as "The Eloquent Peasant" and "The Shipwrecked Sailor" (forerunner of Sinbad) that were to be retold through the ages.

Religion too had a revival of sorts, and the cult of Osiris grew especially strong. At Abydos, where Osiris was supposed to have been buried, passion plays were given by peasants and priests. They re-enacted the god's life, death, and triumph. In elaborate processions, chanting prayers, the worshipers marched to his tomb, adoring the great Osiris.

But shrewd priests profited from this increased devotion. They invented terrifying new dangers that the dead must face in the hereafter, and for which they required priestly spells. The number of these incantations, charms, and mumbo-jumbos grew so vastly that there was no longer room to letter them on coffin walls. Now they were inscribed on a roll of papyrus that was laid in the tomb and was known as the "Book of the Dead." All this, of course, was only for the rich and noble; for the poor, a pit-grave, a pot of food, and perhaps a prayer sufficed.

Yet for all its cultural and material splendor, the great Twelfth Dynasty finally weakened. The last of the line, Queen Sebeknefrure, ruled four years and disappeared from history. During her reign and after it, the unruly lords of the nomes reasserted themselves. One by one each noble seized what power he could, and usurpers arose. Futile dynasties followed, and during the next two centuries the disintegration of the country was complete. We can picture the destruction of dams and reservoirs, the fear of famine; and now, for the first time, the Nile valley was ravaged by invaders.

Near the end of the Fourteenth Dynasty they came, lured by the wealth of Egypt's temples and her now unprotected borders — the Asiatic Hyksos, the "shepherd kings." Entering from the east, they seized the Delta and built a walled city named Avaris. From here they marched up the river, capturing nomes and cities till they controlled the land as far as Thebes. Upper Egypt they held as tributary.

Who were these Hyksos? Perhaps nomads from Arabia, perhaps half-civilized Phoenicians or Syrians, with probably some Hurrian chiefs and horsemen among them. Their kings ruled as Pharaohs, but to the Egyptians they were barbarians; they desecrated shrines and altars, and built nothing of importance. After a century they were driven out. From them Egypt had gained only one thing: the horse-and-chariot combination, to be used with a professional army for her own future conquests.

BEAUTIFUL KNOSSOS

Away from all this turmoil, the city of Knossos, safe on the island king-dom of Crete, was flourishing as the center of a unique and lovely civilization.

Minoan trade and sea power reached their peak in these centuries. Ships from Crete covered the Aegean and the Mediterranean, rivaling those of Egypt and Phoenicia. In her home ports, the vessels of those two countries anchored beside the Minoan fleet at crowded wharves. Nor did ships alone carry her influence. In this period Crete attained a cultural, and in some places perhaps a political domination over the Achaean Greek settlements of the Aegean area — on the mainland, the islands, the coast of Asia Minor. Fashions and crafts in the Minoan style brought a barbaric splendor to the great thick-walled cities of Tiryns and Mycenae, on the plain of Argos in southern Greece, which came under the artistic if not the commercial sway of the Cretans. And similar imitation marks the treasures found in the ruins of the seven cities of Troy.

But it was her wares, above all, that spread the culture of Crete. In the city of Knossos, three and a half miles from the coast — as in other Cretan cities — worked skilled artisans. They made pottery, seals, and jewelry; they worked in gold, silver, and precious stones. Their weavers produced fine cloth, their metal-workers made bronze armor and arms and chariots, and other craftsmen fashioned leather goods and orna-mented harnesses. The Minoans made all these exquisite things, and the ancient world bought them.

It is through her art that we see Crete as she was then. On the frescoed walls of Cretan temples and palaces, in brilliant color, priests and priestesses come before the altars, graceful dancers move across a stage, bullfights are performed in a crowded arena, athletes fight in boxing-rings. This was the aristocratic life of Crete. And in all of it the debonair Cretan ladies moved freely. Pictured in modern-looking dress

LADIES IN CRETE

Three fashionable Cretan ladies are seated on a long bench, having a gay party. With their corseted small waists, puffed sleeves, bell-shaped skirts, lovely tresses falling below their shoulders, and careful make-up, they seem almost modern. Their talk might be about men, tomorrow's bullfight and who would be there, or a temple ceremony to honor the Mother Goddess. Outside, but within call, stands a slim-waisted retainer.

and with much jewelry, they are shown taking important roles in religion, society, and sport — as priestesses, actresses, even women bull-fighters!

These artistic people loved their sea-swept island, and they captured its beauty in the crafts of the middle Minoan period. Gone are the stylized designs imitated from Egypt. Now graceful patterns, drawn from nature's own lines, appear on walls and ceramics. We see realistic

CRETE

Behind this girl of Crete is the beautiful mural that decorated the
throne room in the palace of Minos in Knossos. Unique in design,
Cretan mural subjects range from birds and flowers to bullfights. And
like the wall paintings of Egypt, they show us how the people of this
civilization lived and dressed.

vines, plants, and flowers; bulls, sheep, goats, dolphins, even octopuses
are drawn and painted in action. Here was an art that portrayed, in
movement and grace, the land of Crete and the sea around it.

And during the last Minoan period architecture reached new
heights of elegance and splendor in Knossos and other Cretan cities.
Now, amid ordinary houses and shops of sun-dried bricks, rose beautiful stone temples and many-roomed palaces, impressive arenas, buildings with great flights of steps leading up to them — some as high as
five stories. In the royal theater of Minos the audience was accommo-
dated in a room three thousand feet square! And here bathrooms and
plumbing were used; terra-cotta pipes sealed with cement led to sewers
six feet in diameter.

But Minoan life had its dark side, an undercurrent of mystery and
horror that could be glimpsed in its religion. Like most ancient peo-

ples, the Cretans worshipped nature — mountains, caves, sea, sun, moon, stars; their ancient forests of cedar and cypress were peopled by them with dryads, satyrs, and nymphs that Greek mythology would later borrow. But the frightful natural phenomena of their small island — earthquakes, raging winds, thunder and lightning, storms at sea — must have made the gods seem angry. Their chief divinity, the Great Mother, with her attendant lions and snakes, was the goddess of fertility but also of death. Death was the essence, too, of ceremonies in homage to the sacred bull, the Minotaur of dread fame. Legend told of the yearly tribute of Greek lads and maidens offered to this monster, half-man and half-bull, in his labyrinth. And we have evidence that the Cretans trained captive children for the dangerous ritual sport of bull-leaping. Originally, they doubtless appeased the gods with human sacrifices; and they buried their dead in baked clay coffins or large pottery jars, with food, games, toilet articles, and figurines to comfort them in the dark silence whither they went.

But Crete's situation — a small island in a turbulent world — gave her a more practical reason for fear. The recent deciphering of the Cretan tablets reveals that she was in repeated danger from mainland invaders. And indeed, in less than two centuries, Knossos was to know the full terror of barbarian invasion and be obliterated from the earth.

THUTMOSE III

This is the Pharaoh Thutmose III, the Conqueror—greatest king of Egypt's powerful Eighteenth Dynasty and builder of the New Empire. He fought and ruled for fifty years, and left his son a land extending all the way from Punt to the Euphrates River.

IV.   Clashing Empires—The First Internationalism

1580-1000 B. C.

So far, we have seen brilliant material cultures rise around the Mediterranean: Sumer and Akkad and Babylon, the Pyramid Age and the Middle Kingdom, the Hattian Federation and the isle of Crete. Yet these nuclei of civilization remained far apart. In the next few centuries all that was dramatically changed.

Now a new spirit was abroad — it has been called the "First Internationalism." Populations were increasing; great empires were taking shape and pressing against one another's borders; there were more contacts and interchanges between peoples. Nations traded not only goods but savants and ambassadors, magical cults and literature: poems, myths, treatises, epics were translated from Akkadian into Hittite, Hurrian into Canaanite, Egyptian into Akkadian, and vice versa. On the dark side, to be sure, conquest was rampant and military machines were more dreadful than ever before. And in the wake of armies, slavery was increasing, though perhaps it was preferable to carnage. Yet despite this — or maybe because of it — there were also startling reactions against war and cruelty and superstition. Civilized man had already made strides in that direction: notions of kindness and good will from the chaos of Egypt's Feudal Age, the stern justice of Hammurabi's Code, and the more humane Hittite Laws. But with this new world outlook, man's higher aspirations suddenly blazed into vivid episodes.

Egypt plunged into conquest and became the dominant world power. But the languid Pharaoh Akhnaton turned aside to dream of one god for all men — a benevolent, loving god of sunshine instead of countless grotesque idols — and withdrew to a beautiful city that enshrined his dream.

Hatti reached her widest expansion, and her King Muwatallis won a great strategic victory on the battlefield of Kadesh. But his successor, Hattusilis, followed it with a still greater feat of diplomacy — the first major peace treaty of the Western world.

Tens of thousands of aliens were held in bondage. But Moses led the Israelites across the Red Sea, to receive the Tables of the Law at Mount Sinai and wander on the hard road to freedom and the Promised Land.

Amid the spectacular achievements of the first internationalism, such interludes seem ephemeral. Akhnaton's name and vision were erased after his death; the treaty was an exception; the Hebrew Exodus was not even recorded on Egyptian stelae. Yet, in an age of clashing empires, these flashes of idealism betokened a brighter day for mankind.

THE AGE OF EMPIRE—AND A DREAM

There was nothing idealistic about the splendor and military might of Egypt's New Kingdom. This once peaceful land had learned from driving out the Hyksos invaders; now she had a real army of charioteers, archers, and ax-men. It was the Age of Empire, and the powerful Pharaohs of the Eighteenth Dynasty — most of them bore the names of Amenhotep and Thutmose — added conquest to conquest. They brought to Egypt the riches of Asia and the gold of Nubia, to fill the royal treasury and cover the altars of Amon-Ra. These rulers installed a regime of pomp, glory, grandeur, and ostentatious luxury.

Of them all, none matched the prowess of Thutmose III, the conqueror. He came to power through a familiar dynastic struggle, but this one had a colorful twist to it. His chief rival was a woman, his sister and senior, who kept him in the shade for twenty-two years!

Princess Hatshepsut became *the Pharaoh* after a series of palace revolutions that ousted and sometimes restored her aged and senile father, her two brothers, and herself. In the end she pushed aside the young Thutmose III and assumed the sole rule. During her reign she wore masculine attire and customary false beard, for we see her sculptured as a bearded man in the robes of a Pharaoh. The first eminent woman in history, she kept peace and order in her kingdom, ruled with wisdom and justice, and erected the usual shrines and two gold-topped obelisks at Karnak. On the west bank of the river, near Thebes, she built a beautiful colonnaded temple against the red sandstone cliffs of the Nile, and sent the first fleet to far-off Punt to collect shrubs of myrrh with which the temple gardens were perfumed.

When Hatshepsut died, after ruling more than two decades, her brother — Thutmose III was Pharaoh at last — tried to remove all traces of her. Deeming it "the shame of the Nile" that a woman had ruled Egypt, he had her name erased from her buildings, her statues destroyed, her gold-topped obelisks sheathed with granite.

But more pressing matters—wars and conquests—were to occupy Thutmose III for the rest of his reign. In seventeen campaigns in twenty years, this famous warrior successfully invaded Palestine, Phoenicia, Syria, and Mitanni. Even as he came to the throne, Egypt's outlying provinces revolted. Thutmose promptly took the field, and at Har-Megiddo in May, 1468 B. C., he routed an allied force led by the King of Kadesh. Thence the victorious Pharaoh marched northward, sub-duing cities, exacting tribute, establishing garrisons, appointing gover-nors. But the defeated enemy retreated still faster — one hundred and fifty miles north, to the safety of his walled city on the Orontes River in Syria.

Thutmose III embarked on campaign after campaign. A year was spent organizing his first conquests, then there were five expeditions in five years, and all the ports of Phoenicia and Palestine were in his hands. Next he built a navy and landed his troops at Simyra, a Phoe-nician seaport. From there he marched east twenty-five miles and at long last besieged the fortress city of Kadesh. It surrendered to famine after six months. Now the way was open, and the conqueror paused only to crush an attempted coastal rebellion and then marched on through Syria. City after city fell before assault or quick siege. Finally he reached and crossed the Euphrates, and at Carchemish defeated the King of the Mitanni and his army of horsemen — scattering them far and wide, says the Egyptian report. This flood-tide of conquest Thut-mose III duly marked with a boundary-stone east of the great river.

In ten years the warrior Pharaoh had brought Syria and the coast lands of the Near East under his rule. Such was his fame that Hittite, Babylonian, and Assyrian kings sent him gifts.

To rule this far-flung empire, Thutmose III had to keep his army alert and engage in many more campaigns against revolting petty vas-sals. And when he was past seventy his old foe the King of Kadesh once more incited an allied rebellion. Again the aging conqueror landed at Simyra, marched inland, and captured Kadesh: it was his seventeenth and last campaign. Weakened by age, he made his son co-regent around 1440 B.C., and a few years later he died.

From his many conquests, the great Thutmose had brought back fantastic spoils of war to his capital of Thebes. With this wealth he built new temples and added to the glory of Karnak and the luxury of his court. Above all, he heaped gifts on the altars of Amon-Ra — the riches of the captured cities of Lebanon; the golden vessels of Syria, Mitanni, Phoenicia; and the herds and lands and slaves of Egypt herself. His three warlike successors continued the same course. Their reigns were filled with victories, riches, and slaves and the Priesthood of Amon-Ra gained ever vaster fortunes and power. Egypt had reached her absolute peak of splendor, a magnificence in art and living to compare with any age.

Then, incredibly, it all vanished. Amenhotep IV, better known as Akhnaton, reigned only seventeen years. Yet under him the conquests of Egypt were lost, her lavish temples closed, her whole economy disrupted. For he was a man possessed by a vision.

As usual with visions, it had a basis in his own times. Egypt had become a world power, her horizon no longer bounded by her own narrow valley. And at Heliopolis there had been a revival and purification of an ancient cult that worshiped the sun-disk as sole creator and preserver of the universe. From these elements, the new Pharaoh conceived the revolutionary idea of absolute monotheism. He believed in one god, the life-giving sun, a god of love and mercy for all mankind. Obsessed by the greatness of his concept, he decided that the whole of Egypt must share his joyful belief; men must bring light and life to others, as the sun did to the earth. Recklessly he closed the temples of the rich and corrupt priesthood, abolished state worship of the old gods, had the name of the chief-god Amon erased from his temples and shrines. In its stead he inscribed the name of his one god Aton, whose symbol was the sun.

QUEEN NEFERTITI

The beautiful Nefertiti was the wife of Akhnaton, the dreamer-Pharaoh of Egypt; in a wall inscription he calls her "The great Royal Wife . . . beloved Mistress of the Two Lands." This portrait of her is drawn after a sculpture made by the artist Thutmose (not the Pharaoh of that name), which was found in the ruins of Akhetaton, the sacred city Akhnaton built to his one god Aton. Here the queen is applying green eyeshadow to accent her beauty, while three maids-in-waiting play dulcet music on harp, lute, and oboe.

Changing his name to Akhnaton ("Aton is satisfied"), he left the iniquities of Thebes and built a beautiful new capital called Akhetaton (Horizon of Aton) in his god's honor. Here, religion reformed, he proceeded to free art. With his approval his artists threw off priestly restrictions and introduced a new style that was more realistic, human, and intimate.

But the royal reformer had moved too fast. He had angered a wily priesthood and shocked a believing people, whose many gods had served Egypt well for more than fifteen hundred years. And with the temples closed, the streets were filled with priests and their countless attendants, as well as multitudes of laborers who had been building and repairing shrines. Egypt's largest domestic business had been liquidated.

Her empire went next. Akhnaton, his eyes fixed on Aton, completely neglected military and administrative duties. Unable to believe in conquest, this pacifist failed to answer a thousand pleas for help from the governors of his provinces. Insurrections broke out; bewildered Egyptian garrisons were slaughtered; foreign tributes and taxes ceased.

Ravaged by illness, all Egypt against him, his country in confusion and her territories lost, the dreamer Pharaoh died in 1353 B. C., before he was fifty.

The waiting priests assumed power almost at once. Aton's symbols were cut from every monument, those of Amon-Ra restored. Akhnaton's tomb was despoiled, his name became a word not spoken, his city was abandoned, and once again Thebes was the capital. A few relatives briefly followed the unfortunate Pharaoh on the throne. One son-in-law succeeded him and then disappeared, probably murdered by priests. Another, approved by the priests after he changed his name from Tutankhaton to Tutankhamen, reigned a few years; we care about him only because his magnificent tomb, safely buried by sand, was uncovered in 1922 by the English archaeologists Howard Carter and the Earl of Carnarvon. Last came an obscure distant relative, and then the famous Eighteenth Dynasty ended after more than two centuries.

The death blow was struck by an officer and noble named Harmhab, who became Pharaoh with the help of the army and the priests. His first effort was a pious duty to Amon-Ra. All the temples were reopened and their wealth restored; the high priest of Thebes received a Nubian mine, perhaps as a bonus. Then Harmhab turned to the business of ruling. He stopped extortion and bribery among tax-collectors; he appointed honest viziers, judges, and bureaucrats; he reorganized his government from the Delta to Nubia, and inspected it continually. The old ways were back — but history would remember Akhnaton's dream.

MANY WARS, ONE PEACE TREATY

Conquering Pharaohs were not the only warriors who harried the ancient world during the Age of Empire. Wars of conquest or plunder were the rule on all sides.

Farther east, Babylonia had been stagnant under the half-civilized Kassites. After Hammurabi's death these people, from the Zagros Mountains east of the Tigris, had begun migrating into the Plain of Babylon to seek work as farm laborers. Doubtless welcomed by the rich landowners as cheap labor, the dangerous influx of aliens soon swarmed in like locusts and seized power. For almost six centuries Kassite kings had ruled, and then Babylon changed masters. In 1591 B. C. a Hittite king sacked the city and carried off slaves and cartloads of temple treasures. But the real conqueror was Elam, independent once more and under a new warlike dynasty. In the twelfth century B. C. the Elamite king Shutruk-Nahhunte captured Babylon, overthrew the Kassite ruler to place his own son on the throne, and dragged the statue of the Babylonian great god Marduk to Susa. His successors continued his conquests till Elam's empire stretched from the Persian Gulf north to Ashur, and included the whole Tigris valley, the Zagros range, and all of what is now western Iran.

Meanwhile to the north, a piratical sea people, made up of various nationalities, who were later to terrorize Asia Minor, began their raids by spoiling the greatest prize in the Mediterranean. Charred ruins enable us to imagine the scene.

It must have been a peaceful summer day. In Knossos workmen were busy as usual; there was trading in market-places and shops; women were buying food, children were playing in the dusty streets, and goats were wandering about in search of food. A few guards idled in

STREET IN KNOSSOS

Here is pictured a street in Knossos, filled with muscular, narrow-waisted Cretan men and wasp-waisted women. The ladies are dressed in full skirts and blouses with puffed sleeves, suggesting the styles of the Gay Nineties. Note the strange columns, unique in that they are wider at the top than at the bottom.

doorways, and the music of a flute drifted through a window. On the hill above town a bull fight was going on in the arena, the slim-waisted, aristocratic Cretan ladies and their escorts watched and applauded. In front of a temple incense burned on two tripods, while a procession of chanting priests streamed in, followed by devout worshipers bearing gifts for the gods. Suddenly, in the distance, ominous smoke began to rise against the sea. Then a frantic runner raced toward town on the road from the port, shouting his tidings: Sea raiders had burned the Minoan fleet and seized the port, and were advancing on the defenseless city. Confusion and terror followed. Quickly the roads leading to the hills were crowded with frightened women carrying babies, dragging children and household treasures, leading animals, hoping to reach safety.

Burning and destroying as they came, the raiders finally reached Knossos. The Minoan men fought desperately, but by sunset the city had been plundered and put to the torch. None of the defenders survived; their dead bodies lay in gutters, against smoldering ruins.

The ninety Cretan cities celebrated by Homer shared the same fate. All the refugees were hunted out and killed or destroyed, save a fortunate few who fled by sea. After sixteen hundred years, the Minoans — with no army and no fortifications — had been wiped out in a single assault!

Crete's annihilation was more complete than most. But such scenes were horribly frequent, whether the invaders were Kassites, Elamites, sea raiders, or conquering Egyptians. Syria and Phoenicia were a battleground all through the Age of Empire, and Akhnaton's seventeen years of dreamy indifference brought no real respite.

By now the Empire of Hatti was the dominant power in the Near East. Internally strengthened by a new hereditary-succession law wrung from the council of nobles in 1525 B. C., she had turned to foreign conquests. And at the crowning of Suppiluliumas in 1375 B. C. her southern boundary reached clear to Syria. So when that exhausted Egyptian province rebelled, it was an irresistible invitation. To protect his left flank, King Suppiluliumas at once crossed the Euphrates and scattered the army of the Mitanni horsemen, but instead of butchering their king, he made him an ally. Then, with the Mitanni guarding him against the Assyrians, the "Favorite of the Weather-God" turned south. Carchemish and Damascus, the key cities of Syria, fell quickly, and the province came under Hittite rule. Now Hatti was neighbor to Egypt — the most enlightened empire next door to the oldest one — and the result was the beginning of Western diplomacy.

Already in the Age of Empire there had been embassies between Pharaohs and kings of Assyria, Babylon, and Mittani, bearing letters on cuneiform tablets, caravans of treasure, even foreign princesses for the Egyptian royal harem. But these were semi-tributary dealings. Now, for the first time, great powers established foreign relations.

The astonishing first overture came from Egypt. Suppiluliumas received a cuneiform letter from an Egyptian queen, probably Tutankhamen's widow: "My husband is dead, and I have no son. But thy sons, they say, are many. If thou wilt send me a son of thine, he shall become my husband." At first suspicious, the Hittite king was persuaded by a second letter, and dispatched a royal prince to Egypt. But somewhere near the border, the young man and his guards were killed. The widow too seems to have disappeared, and diplomacy languished for a while.

Then Egyptian-Hittite relations began again, on a war footing. Muwatallis was ruling in Hatti; and in Egypt, Ramses II usurped his brother's throne and began raising a mighty army to regain Syria. In 1296 B. C., at Kadesh on the Orontes River, the two met with equal forces, twenty thousand men on each side. Overconfident and easily tricked, Ramses and half his men were lured into a trap, where they were nearly overwhelmed by the Hittite army. Only the demoralization of the victors, who fell to plundering the Egyptian camp, saved the Pharaoh. He extricated himself, rejoined the rest of his troops, and retreated to Egypt — where mural artists, court poets, and scribes were put to work depicting and hailing Ramses' famous "victory"! But actually Kadesh remained in Hittite hands, and the war dragged into border raids.

Finally, after Hattusilis had succeeded to the Hittite throne, the two "great and mighty" neighbor rulers met and signed the first known peace treaty. It was an offensive and defensive alliance, the text engraved on silver plates, pledging brotherhood and peace for all time! To seal the compact, Hattusilis gave his daughter Ma'atne-frure ("Truth Is the Beauty of Ra") in marriage to Ramses II. Accompanied by her father, the bride left Hattusas with a retinue of nobles and palace guards and a caravan of rich gifts. Banners flying, the cavalcade of peace crossed Syria and Palestine, doubtless watched in wonder, to be met near Thebes by an escort of Egyptian nobles and a full army division. The next day, in a magnificent temple, the Pharaoh of Egypt was united in marriage to the Princess of Hatti by the high priest of Amon-Ra, amid bursts of music and clouds of incense. Nomarchs and court ladies and gentlemen attended the ceremony, and for the public there were great feasts and palm-waving processions and dancing in the streets. Furthermore, the Hittite princess was not banished to the harem but became the First Wife of Ramses — and the treaty actually endured a full seventy years.

But after this single episode of peace the old wars resumed with full savagery, shaking even the great powers. Ever weaker Pharaohs followed the self-advertising Ramses; and the Libyans from the west, who had long raided the Delta, began to penetrate Egypt itself. Only Ramses III, of the Twentieth Dynasty, refought the former battles; he invaded Syria to capture Kadesh, and drove the Libyan invaders out of the Nile valley. But otherwise, the kings became mere puppets of the army of the powerful priesthood of Amon-Ra, a situation that portended disaster.

Hatti fared still worse. Helpless kings succeeded Hattusilis; her allies revolted; the cities on her borders were ravaged by the Assyrians. And from the north, from the Balkans and Thrace, from the forests beyond the Danube, and the trans-Caucasian grasslands, hordes of barbarians with weapons of iron swept through Asia Minor. In 1200 B. C. Hattusas was captured and burned, never to be rebuilt. The "sea people" raided the coasts down to the Egyptian Delta. Mushki, Teucrians, Danuna, these mounted warriors, with their women and children in oxcarts, and vast herds of cattle and sheep and horses, devastated the land. In the end the Hittite empire was swallowed up.

And Babylonia had her own mounting terror. Her erstwhile vassals, the warlike Assyrians, struck west against the Mitanni in the 1300s. And in 1114 B. C., King Tiglath-Pileser I of Assyria girded himself for conquest and seized forty cities, including Babylon. Somehow, the slumbering metropolis awoke. She defeated the invader, pillaged

Ashur, and dragged off its chief god to serve the Babylonian Marduk as a menial. But from then on, her life was different. Extra guards mounted the city's walls, for the fear of rising Assyria was hot in the heart and blood of Babylon.

THE EXODUS

Perhaps the most tragic victims of this endless hostility were the captives, the armies of slaves condemned to a life of sorrow. Yet here too these centuries saw a dramatic exception: the greatest liberation story of all time, the Exodus of the Hebrews from the land of Egypt. Modern scholars, authenticating the Biblical narrative, place it in the reign of Ramses II.

According to Hebrew tradition, Abraham, the patriarch of the Israelites, came from Ur in Sumer on the lower Euphrates. In obedience to a message from heaven, he traveled westward with his family to the land of Canaan — the "promised land," where with God's help his descendants were to build a great nation. But there they found only rocky fields, sandy wastes, little grass, and less water. And finally, seeking food for their flocks, they settled in the rich Nile Delta. Through the centuries they grew and prospered, but foreigners were considered dangerous, so the Egyptians enslaved them and they suffered all the horrors of overwork, brutal overseers, poor food, broken spirits.

Moses, who was to lead them out of this bondage, was born during the time when a harsh law decreed death to every newborn Israelite son. His mother hid him for three months and then, placing the infant in a basket of papyrus reeds daubed with pitch, set him afloat amid the rushes of the Nile. An Egyptian princess rescued him and raised him at court as her own child. But when Moses reached the age of forty, he saw an Egyptian foreman beating an Israelite slave. Enraged, he killed the Egyptian, then fled across the Red Sea into the wilderness of Sinai. Then one day, while tending sheep near Mount Horeb, Moses too received a divine commandment. From a bush that

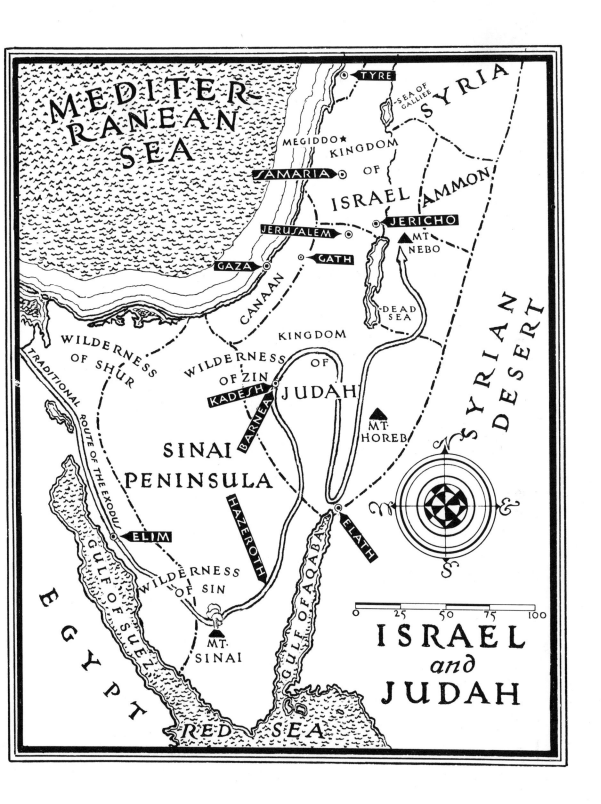

MEDITERRANEAN SEA

TYRE

SYRIA

SEA OF GALILEE

MEGIDDO ★

KINGDOM

OF

ISRAEL

AMMON

SAMARIA

JERICHO

JERUSALEM

MT NEBO

GATH

GAZA

CANAAN

DEAD SEA

WILDERNESS OF SHUR

KINGDOM

OF

JUDAH

WILDERNESS OF ZIN

KADESH BARNEA

SYRIAN DESERT

SINAI PENINSULA

MT HOREB

TRADITIONAL ROUTE OF THE EXODUS

HAZEROTH

GULF OF SUEZ

ELIM

WILDERNESS OF SIN

GULF OF AQABA

ELATH

EGYPT

MT SINAI

0   25   50   75   100

ISRAEL and JUDAH

RED SEA

burned with fire, but was not consumed, came the voice of God order-
ing him to go to the Pharaoh and lead the Israelites out of Egypt.

Reluctant at first, Moses finally returned with his family to Egypt
and terrified Ramses with prodigies and portents. Nine times he promised fearsome plagues that came to pass. Then came the tenth and last
plague, when Yahweh — as the Hebrews called their God — slew the
first-born of all the Egyptians, but safely "passed over" the homes of
the Hebrews, who had marked the lintels of their doors with the blood
of a lamb. Now the frantic Pharaoh summoned Moses and bade him
and the Israelites depart from Egypt.

Guided by a pillar of fire by night and of smoke by day, Moses led
the children of Israel across the Red Sea, which the Lord divided so
they could pass on dry ground. Repenting of his decision, Pharaoh
started in pursuit with an army of chariots and horsemen, but when the
soldiers were halfway across the dry path, the sea rose and drowned
them.

Now began the long wanderings of the Israelites to the "promised
land." After traversing the Desert of Sin, where the Lord fed them with
manna, they camped at the base of Mount Sinai. Moses alone ascended
to the cloud-covered mountain-top, there to commune with Yahweh
forty days and forty nights, and receive the Ten Commandments.

This was the supernatural climax of the Exodus. From then on, the
story was one of human courage and suffering and cruelty — the tra-
vails of the Hebrews to reach and occupy the land of Canaan. The great
Prophet himself was forbidden to enter the promised land, but he was
able to gaze upon it when he ascended Mount Nebo to die at the age
of one hundred and twenty.

His successor, Joshua, led the Hebrews through their battles with
the Canaanites. After Joshua's death the Israelites were ruled by
"judges" who were reputed to be persons of great wisdom and valor.
Among these judges were fascinating personalities: the prophetess
Deborah; Gideon, who led the war against the Bedouins; Jephthah, the
onetime outlaw, who with divine help freed Transjordan and conquered

twenty cities of the Ammonites. Surely the most colorful was the thirteenth judge, Samson. Who has not heard the tales of his great strength? In the end, the temptress Delilah wrung from him the secret of his prowess: his hair had never been cut, in fulfillment of the command of an angel. At last Samson was taken, shorn of his locks and his strength, and blinded by the Philistines. But his hair grew out and his power returned; the blind Samson pushed apart the pillars of the palace of Gaza, giving his life as he slew all the banqueting Philistines.

But the deeds of the judges and the sanguinary conquest of Canaan were only an anticlimax to the great story of the Exodus. Akhnaton's dream of one god lasted only seventeen years. The peace treaty between Egypt and Hatti was kept for three-quarters of a century. But after three thousand years, the Western world still traces its ethical foundations to the triumphant idealism of Mount Sinai.

EARLY GREEKS

Here we see a tribe of Hellenes who have left their forest lands along the Danube and are passing through the rugged mountains of Thessaly to seize the land of the Minoans and Mycenaeans. But this is no peaceful penetration; these warriors are making their way by slow stages toward the sea—killing and destroying. Later, after capturing the royal walled fortresses of Tiryns and Mycenae and enslaving the natives, they settled in the Peloponnesus; and their descendants became the disciplined and defiant Spartans.

V.   Culture from Small Nations

1000-750 B. C.

In the next two hundred and fifty years, civilization spread and sparkled around the Mediterranean by a back route. Mounting wars and anarchy virtually overwhelmed the great powers. But small nations could thrive amid the turmoil: Phoenician navigators sailing unknown seas, long-haired Greeks moving into the Aegean, Etruscans going westward, Hebrew nomads carving themselves a kingdom. It was these "little people" who made the new advances, in a shimmering commerce of goods and ideas. For there were no longer any mighty settled empires to produce monumental achievements as of old.

Egypt went down repeatedly under invasion after invasion. Her story, from the death of Ramses III in 1164 B. C. till her conquest by Cambyses the Persian in 525 B. C., was one of disorder, degradation, and disaster. It was the slow dying of an ancient civilization. Dynasty followed dynasty: first the high priests of Amon ruled; then came the Libyan conquest and kings; then dark Pharaohs from Nubia. With every dynasty, the seat of power changed — Thebes, Heracleopolis, Bubastis, and Sais were capitals in turn. Then again, all the cities were ruled by turbulent nobles. Irrigation canals fell to ruins; architecture and art were nothing but bad imitations of ancient work; only the Book of the Dead grew in size, till some copies were sixty feet long. And this age of decay had its symbol: tomb-robbers were ever busy; tomb-robbing was now a profitable business. In vain the Tanites of the Twenty-first Dynasty tried to halt the sacrilege. Finally the priests gathered together the mummies of ancient Pharaohs from plundered tombs and hid them in an unused burial vault where these sorrowful relics would be safe for nearly three thousand years.

Babylonia's death was imminent too, at the hands of her neighbor Assyria. During all their history the Assyrians had been building a record of callous cruelty. Often after a battle captives were killed by mutilation, flaying, burning alive. Other ancients had such customs, but Assyrian kings enjoyed the brutality in person. And for the Assyrians a city captured was a city razed. All the trees were cut down and the ground sown with salt; all the men, women, and children were killed, unless slaves were needed. Then long, guarded lines of captives would be marched over mountains and plains to Nineveh and cruel servitude. Before 1000 B. C. Assyria was using weapons made from Hittite iron; by 750 B. C. her army was the best armed, best trained, best disciplined in the Near East — a terrible destructive force for her sadistic kings.

And Hatti, of course, was already swallowed up in the Near Eastern anarchy, with barbarian invaders destroying the cities of Asia Minor and ravaging Mesopotamia with *their* new arms of iron.

For this was the beginning of the Iron Age: a holocaust of empires, but a time of opportunity for weaker lands. Cheap tools were available for the first time in history: axes and plowshares for farmers, kits for artisans. It was likewise a new era of cheap maritime transport; and now alphabetic writing could be mastered by any merchant, whereas cuneiform had been limited to specialized scribes. With these advances — iron and improved ships and the alphabet — small countries began to flourish and spring up all around the Mediterranean, spreading old cultures and shaping new ones.

ENTER THE GREEKS

Among the newcomers to civilization were the Greeks, who entered history as long-haired barbarians. Around 1900 B. C. a tribe of Indo-Europeans — they called themselves "Hellenes" — began their slow migration from the Danube forests, over mountains and down valleys, to the many-islanded sea and the mainland of Greece.

Rude folk in sheepskins, driving flocks and herds, these firstcomers were the Achaean Greeks. They probably settled briefly in Thrace; then, seeking better land, they passed through Macedonia and Thessaly and reached the Peloponnesus. Perhaps they were the ones who destroyed Crete. At least we know that they besieged and captured Troy in the famous Trojan War, which is thought to have taken place about 1194-1184 B. C. After them came the Dorians in 1100 B. C., a conquering horde of warriors who swept through the land, devastating the ancient cities of Tiryns and Mycenae, killing, enslaving, destroying. They overran the Achaeans in the Peloponnesus, where they settled to become the ancestors of the warlike Spartans. Next the Aeolians occupied northern Greece. Last of all the Ionians peopled the Aegean Islands, the coast of Asia Minor, and the eastern part of Greece, or Attica; among their descendants would be the Athenians.

By 900 B. C. the Greeks were masters of the surviving Aegean civilization. They had no walled cities or exquisite Cretan-style objects of bronze and gold; but they tended the vines and olive groves, continued making fine pottery, preserved the art of seamanship. Not only that, but they were curious new customers for the Phoenician traders, whose ships had long visited the Aegean beaches to sell their wares to Minoans and Mycenaeans. Now the long-haired Hellenes were hungry for the wondrous goods of Egypt and Asia: cloth, jewelry, pots and pans, glass, beads, armor, helmets, swords and spears. From the Phoenicians they borrowed a garment which they adopted, the chiton. From the merchants of Tyre and Sidon they got the alphabet and learned to read and write. Slowly, surely, on all this heritage of beauty that they found, the Greeks began to build a new culture of their own.

Their small towns grew into cities; their tribal chiefs became petty kings. But, fatally, the Greek city-states never formed a united nation. Set in a land of mountains, cut off by deep ravines, connected to one another only by mountain roads, the cities were self-sufficient units and would always remain so. The Greeks would ever be separated in peace, seldom united even for a war of defense. Athenians were for Athens; Spartans for Sparta; Thebans for Thebes. Only three bonds held them together: their gods, their games, and their literature.

The Hellenes had brought with them a primitive religion of un-numbered gods, headed by the thunder-hurling Zeus. There were gods for sea, land, and sky, for every phase of nature, for every occasion, for every prayer. Soon these quarreling human-like deities were at home in Greece. The mightiest, it was believed, lived on Mount Olympus in Thessaly, and many spoke to their followers through oracles. In dim caverns, or temples over rock fissures, the Greeks sought to find solu-tions to their problems and hope for their future. The holiest oracle, supposedly attended by the god Apollo, was in a place called Delphi at the foot of Mount Parnassus. To oracles or temples, in times of victory or defeat, streamed processions of the devout, who waited outside for the sacred word from within. Only priests could stand before the altar, consult the oracle, interpret the mysteries, bring back the answers of the gods — though, apart from religion, they never attained any power.

An even greater unifying force was the Greek devotion to athletics. The famous Olympic Games began traditionally in 776 B. C. and were celebrated during nearly twelve hundred years. From all the city-states of Greece, from the Aegean Islands and the coast of Asia Minor, from faraway Syracuse in Sicily and Cyrene in Africa, and from every col-ony, freeborn Greek youths came every four years to compete at Olym-pia in Elis during the feast of Zeus. The games opened in a stadium where an orator delivered a patriotic speech praising Greece and her athletes. For five days there were athletic contests of every kind: box-ing, wrestling, foot-races for different distances, and the Pentathlon with its five events — broad jump, discus throw, javelin throw, two-hundred-yard dash, and wrestling match. And in a hippodrome nearby horse races were held, the main one being with four-horse chariots. Victors were crowned with a wreath, cheered and feted and immortal-ized in sculpture and song.

Besides the games at Olympia, others were held at religious festivals in Athens, Delphi, Nemes, Corinth, and Delos. And in some places contests in dancing, speaking, singing, poetry, and playing the harp and flute were added to the athletic competitions.

So it is not surprising that Greece's first great contribution to Western civilization was in epic poetry. Her two great epics, the *Iliad* and the *Odyssey,* were attributed by tradition to the blind poet Homer, but nowadays scholars believe that they were welded out of lays sung by many traveling rhapsodists, the *Iliad* perhaps wrought by a gifted bard named Homer. Both epics show us Greece, half legendary, half real, as she entered history. The *Iliad* sings of "the wrath of Achilles," an episode in the famous Trojan War: it closes in on the ten-year siege of Troy by the Achaeans, that followed the flight of the Spartan queen, Helen, with the Trojan prince, Paris, to give us a magnificent tale of gods and heroes and human passions. And the *Odyssey* relates the fabulous voyage home from Troy of Odysseus, the idealized prototype of the first Greek mariners to sail the dangerous seas.

TRADERS AND COLONISTS

After Greece, more and more new centers of culture began appearing around the Mediterranean. Now many nations were carrying the glittering goods of civilization to near and distant lands. These were the traders and colonists: the Greeks themselves, who became a maritime people; the Syrians with their caravans; the Etruscans, a seafaring people whose home was western Italy; and the most famous navigators of ancient times, the Phoenicians.

Descended from the Semitic Canaanites, the black-bearded Phoenicians had settled on a narrow hundred-mile strip of eastern Mediterranean coastline, between the Lebanon mountains and the sea. Since their territory was too small to support an ever-growing population, they probably learned shipbuilding from the Egyptians and soon took to the sea. At first they sailed uncertainly along known shores by day

GREEK SHIP

With this type of ship the Greeks explored, traded, pirated, and warred. The armed men on its deck suggest war. But even a trading ship needed to be armed to protect herself from enemies or to do a little buccaneering on the side. To make a profit, an ancient vessel carrying merchandise to a foreign port had to return home with a cargo of goods, bought or pirated; and often a few slaves were hidden in the hold.

and beached their ships at night. Eventually they discovered the fixed position of the North Star — the "Phoenician Star," the Greeks later called it — and with this guiding star they sailed boldly across unknown seas. Before 600 B. C. the Phoenicians were mining silver in Spain; they had passed through the Pillars of Hercules — Gibraltar — into the Atlantic Ocean and discovered the islands with tin mines to the north that would one day be called Great Britain; they had sailed along the African coast to the equator, and reached the Azores, six hundred miles west of the coast of Portugal. And by 600 B. C. they had reputedly circumnavigated Africa itself! The Greek historian Herodotus relates the exploit: "The Egyptian Pharaoh Necho . . . sent a fleet manned by a Phoenician crew, with orders to sail west around Africa. . . . These Phoenicians sailed from the Arabian Gulf into the southern ocean, and every autumn put in at some convenient spot on the Libyan [African] coast, sowed a patch of ground, and waited for the next year's harvest. Then, having got their grain, they put to sea again, and after two full years rounded the Pillars of Hercules in the third year, and returned to Egypt [through the Mediterranean]. . . . This is how Libya [Africa] was first discovered to be surrounded by the sea."

These great Phoenician voyages were usually made by traders. Every desperate chance was taken not for glory but for gain. With their ships beached on a sheltered shore, they traded with the natives,

PHOENICIAN TRADERS

On this Attic beach astute Phoenician traders are displaying their merchandise to the Greeks. According to custom, their small ship has been beached. Their goods have been unpacked, and you can see one crafty trader showing a piece of gay cloth to an interested Greek matron. In a box there are swords for the men, and on the ground, pottery for the women.

exchanging metal weapons and tools, bright beads, and gaily colored cloth for ivory, gold, tin, amber, perfumed gums, and other raw materials needed by a growing Mediterranean civilization that they were helping to spread. And to every port and beach they touched, they also brought the news of the world.

Actually, profits were necessary for Phoenicia's survival. Weak in numbers, a small neighbor to great empires, she was forced to depend on diplomacy and gold to protect herself. Total destruction was avoided by paying tribute. This was not a lack of courage — when compelled to, her people fought bravely as in the heroic sieges of Tyre and Carthage — but it was simply a matter of judgment.

For Phoenicia on the coast, and Syria farther inland toward the Euphrates, were both in the path of conquest. Invading armies crossed and recrossed their lands. The rich Phoenician ports of Biblos, Sidon, and Tyre were captured, looted, and rebuilt; so were the Syrian cities of Damascus, Kadesh, and Carchemish. The people of these cities lived in an atmosphere of war and threats of war from the time of Sargon the Great to the reign of the Roman Emperor Augustus. Nevertheless they continued patiently to work and to prosper.

The Syrians too were Semites, and trade was in their blood. But unlike the Phoenicians they were unable to maintain their independence and lived almost always in a state of vassalage. At first a province of Sargon's, Syria had been a vassal in turn of the Babylonian, Egyptian, and Hittite empires. She was overrun by Scythian and Cimmerian nomads, and ravaged by the "sea people." And in the future she was to pass into the hands of Assyria, Persia, Alexander, the Seleucids, and finally Rome — an imposing list of masters.

Yet, through it all, the Syrians continued to work and buy and sell, in order to pay taxes and tributes to their overlords. Perhaps no people were ever more devoted to trade and trade methods than one of their tribes, the Aramaeans. Especially clever, astute, and able, they made themselves indispensable in markets and counting houses as scribes, clerks, and accountants, and they served in various capacities in the offices of conquering kings. Assyrian reliefs show them itemizing plunder, even counting the severed heads of captives so some king might pay off his brutal warriors. And their language, Aramaic, was so simple, so easy to learn and to write, that it became in time the market language of the Near East and the spoken tongue of the common people. For loaded Syrian caravans went in every direction — east across the Zagros Mountains to the Iranian Plateau, north over river fords to Asia Minor, south through the deserts to Arabia and the Delta of the Nile, trading from town to town the goods of the Near East.

By these paths of trade, on land and on sea, civilization was gradually carried to all the known world and beyond. And it spread from the east by yet another means: the planting of colonies in the western Mediterranean. In this enterprise, as in shipping, the adventurous Greeks soon became rivals of the Phoenicians. Little love was lost between them. The Greeks referred to a man of dubious honesty as a "Phoenician"; what the Phoenicians called a dishonest person is not known, but perhaps it was a "Greek"! By 750 B. C. the Greeks were settled in Sicily and edging up the Italian peninsula; and, in the next century and a half, colonies of Greek traders sprang up on every possible beach along the north coast of the Mediterranean — "like frogs around a pond," said Plato. For their part, the Phoenicians became established across the sea on the African coast. According to tradition, in 813 B. C. they built their walled town of Carthage and then proceeded to found their own colonies of traders along the south shore.

Meanwhile an unknown people — the Etruscans, they were to be called — had migrated to northern Italy and taken over the land above the Tyrrhenian Sea and enclosed on the east by the Arnus and Tiber Rivers. Just where they came from is a mystery. Ancient historians said they were from Lydia; and some modern archaeologists think that they were indeed emigrants from the turmoil in Asia Minor, who established themselves as rulers over the prehistoric Iron Age Italians. In that case, they brought with them their priests, their artisans, and their way of life — including the Sumerian arch and vault, and the Babylonian art of reading the future in the liver of a sacrificed sheep! (Other scholars claim they were themselves Italians, who adopted Near Eastern art and divination as a result of early trade.)

Either way, our knowledge of Etruria comes from her tombs. Little remains of her famous cities full of bronze statues; her inscriptions have not yet been completely deciphered; and no literature has survived. But her great burial-places are brimming with treasure for the historian: mausoleums in the form of houses, precious and household articles, and frescoed walls covered with gaily colored scenes of Etruscan life. Here this vanished people may be seen eating, drinking, acting, fighting, hunting, fishing, joining in athletic contests — and enjoying music on every possible occasion. The subjects painted range from Bacchanalian dances to formal architectural patterns, and even paradise and the nether regions are shown. We have proof, too, that they were skilled workers in bronze, making and selling chariots, armor, shields, arms, chains, utensils, urns, statuettes, plates, ewers, and candelabra — though their pottery was crude beside the beautiful Greek ware. And no people was ever so fascinated by the grotesque as the Etruscans. Savage monsters, hideous masks, distorted figures, frightening chimeras, furies, all these abound in their works of art.

Perhaps this passion for grotesquerie came from some of their terrifying beliefs. They feared death and its attendants: Vanth; the implacable goddess of fate, and the demon Charun. They dreaded a last judgment in the hereafter, with the saved going to glory with the gods, but the guilty sentenced to an eternity of torment unless their living friends helped them with prayers and offerings. So their burials featured sacrifices — a ram or a bull, a man for an important person. To dignify a great funeral the human victim might be buried alive instead of being slaughtered; or if further homage was due, a gladiatorial combat to the death was held. Daily life too was superstition-ridden. There was a god or demon for every manifestation, and diviner-priests were always on hand, as in Babylon, to interpret signs and portents — a flash of lightning, a thunderbolt, a flight of birds. But on every Etruscan hearthstone

were also small images of *lares* and *penates,* the gentle guardians of
field and home. Some of these customs — the brutal gladiatorial combats, the fearsome omens, the reassuring lares and penates — would
survive among the Romans. This was Etruria's major achievement: she
would hand on her whole culture, architecture and arts and polity, as
well as superstitions, to an up-and-coming Rome.

But in 750 B. C. Rome was only a village on the Tiber, twelve miles
south of the rich Etruscan city of Veii, whereas Etruria was an expand-
ing league of twelve important city-states, united for mutual protection
under a king or dictator. Before the sixth century B. C., the Etruscans
had crossed their river boundaries, built Rimini in the north, established Ravenna over the Apennines on the Adriatic coast, and settled
Capua to the south. From beyond the River Po the barbarian Gauls
watched their growing riches with greedy eyes, while from Sicily and
southern Italy the Greek colonists traded with them and taught them.
Etruscan art began to lose its Asian form and detail and acquired the
staring eyes, rope-like curls, and enigmatic smiles of archaic Greek
sculpture. Likewise the Etruscans either borrowed the half-human
gods of the Greek pantheon and gave them Tuscan names, or else
found counterparts among their own deities—Tini was Zeus, Uni was
Hera, Turms was Hermes, Turan was Aphrodite. Meantime, across the
sea in Africa, the Carthaginians dominated the western Mediterranean
and had closed the Pillars of Hercules to the shipping of the world.

JERUSALEM THE GOLDEN

Back in the eastern Mediterranean a new nation had arisen. The
Hebrew Kingdom came into being in this era, under two great kings
who made their capital world-famous. Jerusalem was first known as
the "City of David," after the founder of the royal house of Israel; but
under his successor, the fabulous Solomon, people renamed it "Jerusalem the golden."

The Bible relates the establishing of the kingdom with special emphasis on the appealing figure of David. History knows few more romantic stories than the rise to royalty of this shepherd, "ruddy, and withal of a beautiful countenance, and goodly to look to." We meet him first after Samuel, sixteenth and last of the judges or priest-rulers, had anointed Saul to be the first king of the Hebrews; but (in the ancient Biblical language) the Lord repented of this and had Samuel anoint young David. Thenceforth the lad was Saul's harpist and armor-bearer; next, he was the Judean champion who slew with a stone from his sling the fearsome Philistine giant Goliath, a monster standing six cubits and a span, or nearly eleven feet tall! From then on David served Saul faithfully, fighting at his side in battle, soothing his troubled hours with song. He married one of Saul's daughters, and a great friendship grew up between him and Saul's son, Jonathan. But David's mounting fame, his youth, his bravery and success in war, the adulation of the Judeans —all this "made Saul very wroth." Afflicted with spells of madness, Saul sought again and again to take David's life. He threw javelins at him, sent him to war in hopes he would be killed, hired assassins to murder him in his bed. Finally, warned by the devoted Jonathan, David fled to the wilderness and joined a band of outlaws and eventually went to Philistia to serve under the King of Gath. But in the end Saul, with Jonathan and two other sons, died fighting the Philistines on Mount Gilboa, and David was at long last anointed by the elders of Judah and Israel.

King David was now ruler of the united kingdom. His army soon attacked and captured the mighty fortress of Zion, Jerusalem, which became the seat of his government and the religious center of the Hebrews. A great fighter, David won many wars against troublesome Philistia and Moab, defeated various Canaanite tribes, was successful against the Syrian kingdom of Zoban, recovered his eastern border on the Euphrates, and ultimately established the Kingdom of Israel as the dominant power in Palestine. But his personal life was stained by his adulterous love for Bath-Sheba, whom he married after having her husband disposed of in battle. And his latter years were saddened by the insurrection and death of his beloved son Absalom. Nonetheless, in their traditions the Israelites accounted him *the* King, just as they considered Moses *the* Prophet.

Solomon the Wise, second son of David and Bath-Sheba, succeeded to the throne and ruled for forty years. It was said that at the beginning Solomon asked God for "a wise and understanding heart"; and the Lord gave him wisdom, and also riches and honor which he had not asked for. Early in his reign he began to build a temple, his most noted achievement. The work took seven years, and into it went all the riches of the then known world. Here were the finest of woods, cedar, ebony, olive, as well as marble, ivory, and bright brass. Gold was used everywhere, with florid Oriental taste. Designs of lions, cherubim, palm trees, pomegranates, and lilies were engraved on the gold-encrusted walls. All the candlesticks and altar vessels were of solid gold. Compared to the shrines of Babylon and Thebes, the Hebrew temple was not large: it was one hundred and five feet long, thirty-five feet wide, and fifty-two and a half feet high. But its magnificence was unsurpassed, and the dedication brought a joyful gathering of the tribes. Priests brought in the Ark of the Covenant wherein were the two tablets given Moses at Sinai; there was a gigantic sacrifice of sheep and oxen, and a prayer by the king; and, the Hebrews believed, fire from heaven lit the altars, and the glory of God filled His house.

In the temple-building and in the vast trade that afterward occupied him, Solomon's great friend and business partner was Hiram the Phoenician, King of Tyre. Hiram supplied bronze, brass, gold, and Lebanon cedar for the temple. In return, the delighted Solomon gave him twenty Galilean cities, a gift that displeased Hiram, for he called them "towns of dirt." But their joint ventures prospered, and their ships and caravans traded everywhere. Solomon's fleet on the Red Sea, manned by Phoenician seamen, brought him as much as four hundred and twenty talents of gold. And every three years Hiram's sailors returned, bringing to Solomon gold, silver, ivory, apes, and peacocks from far-off lands. In time Solomon became known as not only the wisest but also the richest king in the world, and his fame traveled far beyond the Euphrates.

Once, according to the story, the beautiful Queen of Sheba, drawn by tales of his wisdom, came from the East with a long caravan of camels, bearing him gifts. Seated before the great monarch, she asked many questions, and Solomon, on his gold and ivory throne, gave her true answers. After she had seen Solomon's glory and complimented him on the magnificence of his court, his justice, and the blessings of his God, she gave him one hundred and twenty talents of gold, and also precious stones and spices. In return Solomon gave Sheba's queen whatever she asked from his royal treasury. Her visit finished, the queen left the royal house of Solomon, riding on camel-back through Jerusalem's narrow streets, out the eastern gate, past Solomon's great stables, and down the road to Sheba (Southern Arabia). The Bible does not tell us whether she got the alliance she probably came to seek.

So Solomon ruled in Asian splendor. The world's luxuries were served at his feasts, his country was at peace, and he enjoyed his great house and his thousand wives and concubines. But many of them were alien princesses, and he built them shrines before which they could worship their pagan gods, Astaroth, Molech, Chemosh, Baal, Amon-Ra. It was even rumored that the anointed Solomon himself sometimes knelt at these strange altars. All this was considered by the elders an abomination before God. Thus, sinfully and extravagantly, King Solomon lived out his days, and sages then and scholars now have questioned his wisdom.

For he left a bankrupt land and a people about to revolt. After his death the kingdom broke into two parts, never to be reunited. An Egyptian Pharaoh captured and despoiled "Jerusalem the golden." And the reigns of the petty kings of Judah and Israel were a tragic tale of foreign and domestic wars, assassinations, usurpations, bribery, and the worship of Baals or idols. Through all this, prophets walked and talked with God, approving and condemning kings. The greatest was Elijah,

JEWISH SHEPHERD

A lonely shepherd tends his sheep in the sparse, rock-cluttered fields of Judah. He is a tent-dweller. In the distance you can see the tent in which he lives and worships his god, Yahweh. When the grass becomes scarce, or withered by a long dry spell, he moves his flocks and tent and family across the hills to a greener valley.

of whom marvels were told: how he was fed by ravens, how he was carried off to heaven in a fiery chariot. But other prophets predicted dire days to come, when the children of Israel would cherish the memory of David's kingdom and the temple of Solomon.

JUDAH

This Judean prophet, in the rude sheepskin of a shepherd, has left his tent in the desert and come to Canaan, bringing the word of Yahweh to the ungodly. Here on a street corner, thundering prophecies and curses, he calls on the worshipers of Baal to leave their false gods and their misgotten wealth and return to the ancient faith. Raising his hands, he warns the Canaanites of the coming of the Assyrians—a scourge of God, to punish them for their sins and destroy their city.

VI.   "The Assyrian Came Down"

750-550 B. C.

It was not only small nations that took advantage of the confusion in the early Iron Age. The next two centuries were marked by the rise and fall of the brutal and coldly efficient Assyrian Empire, the largest the world had yet known.

After seventeen hundred years of preparation, Assyria at last reached her pinnacle—absolute dominion over a chaotic, crumbling Near East. Then she was utterly destroyed, and the whole world applauded. For her history as a nation was dedicated to bloodshed in its most cruel forms. True, her capital lay in the path of barbarian tribes from the north and of hostile invaders from all sides; from earliest times, battles had raged on the Plain of Shinar. But with the Assyrians war became a business, a way of life, a road to wealth and glory.

Yet this war-driven nation also added something to the ways of peace, both in art and administration. Her heartless relocation of entire populations from one land to another did cause a commingling of races and cultures. And she established the first well-organized cosmopolitan empire—the "Oriental monarchy" with its elaborate system of strict provincial administration that was a model for the later Persian Empire. And her sculptors made magnificent bas-reliefs, miles upon miles of them that adorned the walls of Ashur, Nineveh, and Dur-Sharrukin. Unfortunately for her fame, they glorify her terroristic methods of conquest: countries invaded, plundered, enslaved, laid waste, with the most revolting butcheries. It was only fitting that in the end Assyria herself was erased from the earth by vengeful vassals allied with new invaders.

But the hated Assyrian Empire, by her very existence, had made a real contribution. She preserved and unified ancient Mesopotamian civilization during a time of chaos when it might have been wiped out by barbarian inroads. She spread that civilization—by her armies and settlers, her roads and commercial caravans, her silver shekels and exploitation of Armenian iron mines—farther than it had ever gone before. Thus Assyria held and enlarged the civilized stronghold, in spite of her own lapses into barbarism, and unwittingly prepared the way for better successors.

For when the shadow of Nineveh lifted, Babylon attained her last great age of splendor before she saw the handwriting on the wall at Belshazzar's feast. And meantime other lands—Persia to the east and

Greece and Rome to the west—were laying the foundations of future eras that would carry cultural achievements and administrative skill and even military might to heights undreamed of by the Assyrians.

THE GRIM STORY OF ASSYRIA

The Assyrian Empire reached its peak under the four great kings of the Sargon dynasty, whose combined reigns covered ninety-six years, from 722 to 626 B. C. By that time it stretched from the Persian Gulf to the Mediterranean and was composed of many vassal states—Elam, Babylon, Syria, Phoenicia, Palestine, and even Egypt.

These conquests were achieved by a military machine such as the

ASSYRIAN WAR CHARIOT

War was the business of the Assyrian kings and their god, Ashur, and they really worked at it. Here the great King Sennacherib, with his driver, rides across an Assyrian plain in his chariot, trying out a new bow. Behind him is his long spear. From his belt hangs his sword, and on the side of the chariot is a quiver of arrows. Fully armed, he exercises for war.

WINGED BULL

Setting out past a colossal human-headed winged bull—one of two that guarded the main gateway of his palace at Dur-Sharrukin—the Assyrian King Sargon II and a favorite wife enjoy a chariot ride on the broad surrounding terrace. Four guards stand at attention as royalty passes.

ancient world had never known; its deadly efficiency is still studied today. Assyria had a professional army equipped with weapons of iron. And her invasions were not haphazard marches into hostile territory or heedless dashes into unknown lands. They were carefully planned. In every country there were Assyrian spies, and they often sent information to Nineveh about political and social crises that disturbed enemy states. They reported what grievances were held against kings, and

which captains could be bought. They learned the climate and topog-
raphy of a place, where to build roads and cross rivers. Before the
Assyrians invaded a country they were well prepared. Only then would
ruthless kings lead their charioteers, cavalry, infantry, archers, sappers,
and long lines of camels and pack-mules loaded with food and battle
equipment, to another victory for the triumphant emblem of the war
god Ashur.

Assyria's bloody age of splendor began with Sargon II, who had
taken the name of the famous ancient king of Sumer-Akkad. Her neighbors had fallen long since; then the hosts of Tiglath-Pileser III overran
Urartu (Armenia) and in 732 B. C. seized rich Damascus and the fat
profits of the Aramaean traders. But Sargon started the real westward
sweep. He re-invaded Syria and destroyed Carchemish, once a city-
state of Hatti. Next he conquered Samaria, the Israelite capital of
Palestine, and raided that unhappy land. Now, with slave labor and the
spoils of war, he returned to Assyria and built himself a new capital,
more magnificent than Nineveh: Dur-Sharrukin, the "Fortress of Sargon." He constructed temples, palaces, terraces, walls, bas-reliefs,
winged bulls, walled gardens—and a zoo!

All Assyrian kings built zoos, for in those days the great plain of
the Two Rivers, the mountains of Asia Minor, the Iranian Plateau, and
indeed the whole of the Near East was still filled with great beasts.
There were elephants, lions, panthers, wild bulls, wild boars, buffalos,
wolves, ostriches, snakes, antelope, and deer. The Assyrian kings were
mighty hunters of this game, and their feats were depicted by their
sculptors and proudly recorded by their scribes. One monarch, Ashurbanipal, killed three hundred and seventy lions, thirty elephants, and
two hundred and fifty-seven other wild animals with his own hand.
Many zoo cages were filled with captured lions that were let loose to
be hunted by kings and nobles on horseback or in chariots, for lion-
killing was the privileged sport of the brutal kings of Assyria.

Sennacherib, second ruler of the famous dynasty, was perhaps the
most bloodthirsty. Faced with a mammoth revolt, he embarked on a

LION-HUNTER

The great hunter King Ashurbanipal of Assyria is shown killing a lion. This was truly the sport of kings, for in Assyria only the king could hunt the lion—though he might, in a gracious mood, grant permission to a favorite. Since African lions were larger than those of Asia, they were imported by Assyrian kings, to provide even greater sport.

historic campaign of slaughter. He crushed rebellious Elam and turned west to defeat the united armies of Egypt and Palestine. Then, after his army had suffered a plague which the Jews regarded as an act of God, he went on to ravage the coast, capturing the Phoenician cities of Sidon and Tyre and besieging the Aramaean capital, Damascus. On this expedition, his scribes boasted, he destroyed eighty-nine cities and eight hundred and twenty villages, and sent to slavery in Nineveh two

ASSYRIAN SLAVES

During the great period of Assyrian power (722-626 B. C.) this scene
was common on every road leading into that brutal land. Here is
shown part of a long line of bound prisoners who have crossed the
Euphrates and have still to drag their weary bodies a hundred and
fifty miles more to reach the Tigris.

hundred and eight thousand captives! Meanwhile Babylon had revolted. Sennacherib hurried back, broke through the city's walls, and
did not stop till every vestige of Babylonian life was destroyed. Gods,
palaces, and temples were overthrown, and the waters of the Euphrates
were diverted to flood the streets. Save for a few who escaped, every
man, woman, and child was killed. The ancient capital of Hammurabi
was left a morgue.

With the rich booty of his wars, Sennacherib rebuilt Nineveh, "the
bloody city of lies and robbery." He erected a great aqueduct to bring
cold water from the mountains to his capital; he minted half-shekels of

Those who sicken will be left to die; perhaps sixty per cent will survive. In the rear, carefully guarded, are wagonloads of captured treasure for the priests of Ashur. At the head of every line of captives marched captains from whose necks hung the severed heads of conquered kings—a typical Assyrian touch!

silver, the earliest coins. During his reign Nineveh grew until its protective walls were eight miles long.

A favorite younger son, Esarhaddon, succeeded him—though only after the evil Sennacherib was murdered by his angry older sons. Esarhaddon continued the fighting, defeating ever-rebellious Egypt and cruelly punishing Phoenicia. Yet he made some amends for his father's brutalities: he rebuilt Babylon, and he sent food to Elam when she suffered a famine.

But grim Assyria reached her height under his successor, Ashurbanipal. This ruthless monarch refought all the old familiar wars, suppressing a new rebellion in Egypt, devastating Elam and feasting in

ASHURBANIPAL

In his garden King Ashurbanipal of Assyria reclines in luxury while his plump wife gazes at him admiringly from a nearby chair. Ladies-in-waiting gently wave fly switches to keep insects from feasting on royalty, as another court lady soothes an undoubtedly savage breast with soft music.

company with the severed head of the Elamite king, putting down a revolt by his own brother in Babylon and once again ravaging that ancient city. Still, Ashurbanipal brought some peace and order to his vast empire. He ruled by the typical Assyrian system: his conquered lands were divided into small provinces, each under a governor directly responsible to the king; and he added to the network of military roads that supplied his distant garrisons and promoted commerce. A famous builder, he commissioned many of the most beautiful alabaster bas-reliefs, of animals, gods, kings, and warriors—his own pleasures and iniquities were shown in a lively way. Most remarkable, he built a great library and collected in it the cuneiform writings of Sumer, Elam, Babylon, and Assyria. He bought and borrowed them from temples and palaces, from priests and kings, from everyone and everywhere. After he had them copied, perhaps he returned the originals to their owners, but this seems unlikely. The tablets were carefully catalogued, numbered, and arranged. Here for the first time in history was an all-inclusive library where a scholar could read the story of his world: its history, astronomy, religion, business, medicine, and literature—including epics, myths, moral stories, wise sayings, even puns and riddles!

But Ashurbanipal's work was short-lived. He died in 626 B. C., and fourteen years later Nineveh and the great library were destroyed.

Assyria fell before a combination of nomads that had invaded the Near East. Two of these peoples were half-civilized Indo-Europeans, the related tribes of Medes and Persians. Migrating from the grasslands north of the Caspian Sea, across rivers and swamps, through dark forests and deep ravines, the Medes traversed the Elburz Mountains to enter the Iranian Plateau and build their town of Ecbatana. Their Persian cousins followed and settled near the ancient kingdom of Elam. Down from the north, too, swept the savage Scythian and Cimmerian horsemen, while up from Arabia came the Chaldeans, a young and virile Semitic tribe that took over worn-out Babylon. All of them attacked Assyria, but at first they were disunited and quarrelsome: the barbarians raided alone; the Medes conquered the Persians; the Scythians slaughtered their Median allies; the Chaldeans fought unaided. So their early invasions were turned back, though King Cyaxares of Media did capture and destroy Ashur. But at last the Medes signed an alliance with the Chaldeans; the treaty was sealed by the marriage of Nebuchadnezzar, the Babylonian heir, to Amytis, granddaughter of the Median king. Then the allied rulers, joined by the Scythians, moved in for the kill.

Nineveh and Dur-Sharrukin were captured and totally destroyed. Assyria was blotted from the map. In the words of the Hebrew prophet Nahum: "O king of Assyria . . . thy people is scattered upon the mountains, and no man gathereth them." The mighty Assyrian Empire was divided among the victors. Paid in loot, the Scythians retreated to their lands around Lake Van; the Medes gained the Iranian Plateau, Persia, and Asia Minor east of the Halys River; while to the Chaldeans went Elam, Syria, Phoenicia, Palestine, and the place where Assyria had been.

NEBUCHADNEZZAR'S BABYLON

Nebuchadnezzar, of Biblical fame, ascended the throne of Babylon in 604 B. C. With Assyria gone, his ancient capital was now the center of the Chaldean Empire, and it enjoyed one last burst of prosperity.

Like a proper king, he rebuilt the city. He made temples, gates, and palaces, all of oven-baked brick faced with colored enameled tiles. On the back of each brick was stamped this advertisement: "I am Nebuchadnezzar, King of Babylon." In addition, he repaired irrigation and road systems, and he dredged the Euphrates till it was again navigable from Babylon to the Persian Gulf.

Once more Babylonian commerce and religion flourished, for the two were inseparable. In Babylon a temple was a place not only of altars and idols but of vaults and safes. It was meant to hold gold, letters of credit, records of loans, mortgages, bills, and notes—in fact everything that pertained to profit and loss. The priests of Babylon had a banking monopoly, and temples were everywhere. A contemporary list gives us their astonishing number: fifty-three temples and fifty-five shrines to Marduk, three hundred shrines to earth divinities, six hundred to heavenly divinities like Shamush the sun-god, one hundred and eight altars to the goddess Ishtar, one hundred and eight altars to Nergal of the nether regions and Adal, god of divination, and twelve altars to minor gods, making a grand total of one thousand and eighty!

NEBUCHADNEZZAR

On the terrace of the Hanging Gardens of Babylon sits Nebuchadnezzar, his Median wife beside him. Some guards are seen on a lower terrace, and far in the background rises the Tower of Babel. Nebuchadnezzar built the Hanging Gardens for this princess, to console and remind her of the cool, forested mountains around Ecbatana, where she had spent her youth.

The larger temples teemed with attendants: guards to protect treasures and stop brawls; slaves to scrub and polish; priests for various duties, exorcists, chanters, diviners, magicians; minor officials such as brewers, confectioners, bakers to make sacred cakes for the ceremonies; and, most celebrated, priest-astronomers to scan the clear skies, trying to read man's fate. The very word "Chaldean" came to mean astrologer. For Babylonian priests prepared tablets of fixed stars, dated the winter and summer solstices, plotted the orbits of sun and moon and planets,

and forecast eclipses. Theirs was a religion of stars and magic, of idola-
trous rites and endless darkness after death, of money and banking!

As for the rest of Nebuchadnezzar's Babylon, perhaps we can picture it better if we take a trip there with a merchant of the time. . . .

On a day in Kislef (December), a man named Halab stood outside
the ancient walls. A visitor from Haran on the Euphrates, he had come
to town on business. His small caravan was settled in a compound, and
he and his steward were about to enter the sprawling city. They crossed
a moat, passed through an outer gate, and then strode through one of
the many gates in the massive new inner walls (so wide you could drive
two four-horse chariots abreast on the ramparts). Now they were in
Babylon! Before them was the ziggurat, a seven-storied temple—the
Tower of Babel?—that rose 288 feet, and was crowned with Marduk's
shrine. And far beyond they saw the famous Hanging Gardens, every
terrace bright with exotic flowers and green trees and refreshed by
water from the Euphrates. Now, finding a caravansary, they took quarters, bathed and dressed in fresh robes, and went out to see the sights.

It was a festival day, and Halab was a person of consequence with
proper credentials, so they were admitted to the royal grounds. The
gorgeously appareled king and queen, attended by priests and courtiers, were just coming through the enameled gates of Ishtar, the "gates
of the yellow lions." Halab watched them pass along an avenue of
noble palms on their way to worship in a temple of Marduk.

Now the two tourists left the royal precincts and strolled along one
of the broad highways that divided the city into rectangles. A long
procession of worshipers went by, mostly women, bound for a temple
of Ishtar, goddess of fertility. There were hundreds of them, bearing
images and doves and gifts, led by chanting priests, moving sinuously
to the sounds of crashing cymbals, blaring trumpets, tinkling tam-
bourines.

Picking their way through the milling crowd on the avenue, the
merchant and his steward turned a corner into a crooked, narrow, un-
paved market street. Here in a bedlam of noise were traders from

Egypt, Ethiopia, Asia Minor, Syria, Greece—all shouting and gesticu-
lating. The visitors moved on, staring at fortune-tellers, sellers of songs,
scribes, priests, making way for the camel caravan of a blackbearded
Arabian sheik, pushing past dark recesses of booths and shops, and
peering at the wares within. Food was jumbled against moldering
walls: vegetables, fruit, cheeses, fish, poultry, but little meat. In one
stall an elderly merchant and his wife were selling beer and wines, the
beer from barley, the wine from the juice of the grape and the palm.
Under awnings they saw the famous cloth of Babylon displayed beside
brass braziers, leather articles, pottery, jewels, weapons—everything
that the world's skilled artisans knew how to make.

Exhausted by the noise, heat, dust, and smells, the sightseers went
to stand on Nebuchadnezzar's stone bridge across the Euphrates in the
middle of town. There they enjoyed the cool river breeze and watched
boats loading and unloading on the busy wharves. All along the river
stretched the great warehouses from which the merchandise of Babylon, they knew well, was carried by boat and caravan. North it went, to
Greece and Asia Minor; west to Syria, Palestine, Phoenicia, and Egypt;
south to the oases in the Arabian desert; east to Elam, the Persian
Plateau, and India. Each bale, they noted, stood tied and sealed, with
its invoice written on a clay tablet in cuneiform. A duplicate invoice
was filed in the merchant's office.

Well, tomorrow was a business day for them too. So the tired merchant and his steward returned to the caravansary to eat and get a good
night's sleep.

Early the next morning Halab, a businessman now, called at the
temple of the moon-god Sin to arrange his credits. He was fortunate in
transacting his affairs with the banker-priest pleasantly and promptly,
to the satisfaction of both. Before he left, the priest informed him that
tonight King Nebuchadnezzar was to give a great feast in his palace
hall. Would not the merchant from Haran attend as his guest? Overwhelmed, Halab bowed low and accepted.

At the appointed hour Halab and his host entered the great hall,

BABYLONIAN MARKET

In this picture and the facing one you see a market place in Babylon, crowded with traders from the Mesopotamian valley, from Asia Minor, from far-off Egypt, and even from Punt. All are buying, selling, and shouting; pandemonium reigns.

which was bedecked with banners and perfumed with incense. There sat Nebuchadnezzar himself in Median robes, majestic on his throne of gold and ivory, surrounded by his many wives. Below the dais the members of his court were seated at long tables, and among them the merchant and the priest found places. Trays and compotes of fruit weighted the boards: melons, pomegranates, peaches, plums, apricots, figs, and dates. Gold and silver wine cups were kept filled from great flagons. From guest to guest, waiters carried large square trays heaped

In the markets of Babylon one met the world, learned the news of wars and the death of kings and new gods, and heard strange tales from unknown lands. During the reign of Nebuchadnezzar, Babylon was the center of fashion and religion.

with beef and vegetables, heavily spiced. Blazing roasts of lamb were held high on skewers; roasted peacocks, ducks, geese, and fish caught in the river that morning were set before the diners. Last came the famous sweetmeats of Babylon. Finally, when they had feasted a long time, the grand vizier gave a sign of dismissal. Bowing his thanks, a dazzled Halab bade farewell to his host and returned to the caravansary.

Homeward bound the next day, Halab was still in a daze. That morning he had consulted a fortune-teller to make sure the day was propitious, and paid a handsome fee for his small caravan to travel in the protection of a large one. Now he jogged along the Euphrates road, absently studying the irrigated barley fields of the large estates and calculating the fine harvest. But his mind happily reviewed his trip to Babylon. What a business and social success! He could hardly wait to get home and tell it all to his family. Banqueting with King Nebuchadnezzar had been the great experience of his life.

THE NEWCOMERS

But Babylon was doomed. For the conquest of Assyria had released a black whirlwind from which a single country, Persia, would rise like a jinni to rule the Near East.

None of the three victorious nations retained power. The Scythians chose to stay nomads, living on the steppes of Eurasia, from where they could raid empire after empire for centuries. The Medes, once fierce mounted archers, abandoned themselves to dissolute luxury. Finally, their effeminate King Astyages was deposed and his throne seized by the Persian prince Cyrus. Babylon too declined under a new monarch and his son, the Biblical "Belshazzar." His fall was eagerly awaited by a small group of exiles—the entire surviving Hebrew population, whom Nebuchadnezzar had carried into "Babylonish captivity" when he razed Jerusalem after its second insurrection. It was their prophet Daniel who interpreted the awesome words MENE, MENE, TEKEL UP-HARSIN, written on the wall by a supernatural hand during a royal feast. The warning was swiftly fulfilled. Cyrus, commanding the joint Median-Persian army, marched triumphantly north and west, conquering all Asia Minor; and in 540 B. C. he appeared before Babylon. There was only a token fight—it was rumored that traitorous Babylonian priests had invited him—and then the brass gates were opened for Cyrus the Persian.

So ended—for historical purposes—the ancient culture of Sumer. And the other ancient home of Mediterranean civilization was about to go down too. Free from the constant threat of Assyrian invasion, Egypt enjoyed one last period of feverish brilliance under the Twenty-sixth Dynasty, founded by the Pharaoh Psamtic. But this was a graceful half-Greek sort of flowering; the great days of pyramids, colossal statues, gilded obelisks, colonnaded courts, were past. In thirty centuries Egypt's arts and learning had enriched every part of the ancient world; now her time as an independent nation was done. She too would fall to the Persian, not the humane Cyrus but his mad son Cambyses, who would wreak an insane destruction of the ancient valley of the Nile.

For the newcomers were rising—Persia in the east, and to the west the two young nations of Greece and Rome.

By 750 B. C. the Greek political scene had changed. Weak kings were overthrown and city governments fell to the aristocrats; this was the Age of Nobles. Land was wealth, and most of it was concentrated in their great estates. Only they could train for war and afford armor and horses—and with their booty, they grew richer still at piracy! But these rich gentlemen were harsh and greedy rulers, and their era ended in a revolution.

The tide of unrest rose slowly. Oppressed peasants lost their farms and chose to emigrate to free and fertile lands on the shores of the Black Sea or southern Italy. Those who stayed became sullen masses. And meanwhile new groups arose to challenge the nobles. Increased shipping and the use of money created a new-rich class of traders; defense passed from knights to *hoplites,* or common soldiers. In time, bloody revolts broke out, with the rebellious peasants joined by merchants and artisans and often led by a discontented aristocrat. If this new leader succeeded in seizing power he became a "tyrant"—originally the term meant merely one who took over illegally, and the office was not hereditary. The rise of tyrants began around 650 B. C., and in the next century many appeared in Greece and her colonies.

Athens felt the changes rather late, but in her reforms and political advances she far outstripped her sister-states. The great lawgiver

Solon was named *archon* (leader) with extraordinary power in 594 B. C., just when Attica faced financial disaster. The peasant-farmer was land-less or burdened by a heavy mortgage, and grinding poverty was the lot of the laborer. Solon now rewrote the laws: all mortgages were can-celed, and a limit was put on the amount of land a noble could hold; any citizen might appeal a lawsuit before a jury; and every man became equal before the law. Solon's wise provisions saved Athens from a social revolution. And his successor and relative, Pisistratus—even though he seized office by force—continued the reforms. He reorganized land ownership, dividing the lands of the state and of exiled nobles among the poor; also he strengthened the navy and commerce, rebuilt brick temples with stone and marble, and began attracting artists and scien-tists to the city. His death was followed by a period of confusion and civil war. But finally a noble named Cleisthenes led a successful popu-lar rebellion, and then revised Solon's constitution to place final authority in a representative council and an assembly of elected citizens from all walks of life. This aristocrat had established the first true democracy.

The Athenian Assembly met in the open air in a field called the Pnyx, west of where the Acropolis now is. From a three-step platform politicians or statesmen addressed the citizens as they sat on the ground. Here the important questions of Athens were argued and voted; here peace or war was decided. And here once a year Athenians might, by secret ballots written on pieces of broken pottery—ostrakons —and placed in voting urns, banish or "ostracize" anyone they thought dangerous to the state. Self-government had begun.

Rome, meanwhile, was undergoing a political evolution of her own. According to legend, that little Tiber village, destined to be mis-tress of the world, was founded in 753 B. C. by Romulus and Remus, twin sons of the god Mars and a vestal virgin. (Their mother was supposedly descended from Aeneas, Venus's son, who had fled burning Troy.) Abandoned as infants, suckled by a she-wolf, raised by a shepherd, the young heroes returned safely to build their town, only to quarrel with each other. Remus was slain, and the city was ruled by Romulus and named for him.

Rome's early history is a mixture of fact and fantasy: the disappearance of Romulus in a black cloud, the stealing of Sabine women as wives for the local rabble who were the first settlers, the next three kings named by tradition. What is known is that the Tarquins, of Etruscan—and Greek—lineage, ruled Rome for a century. One of them, Servius Tullius, joined the plebeians and was immensely popular. But Tarquinius Superbus, "the proud," earned such hatred that the Senate deposed him when he was absent at war. His successor outraged Lucretia, wife of the respected Collatinus, and she committed suicide. When the tragedy was reported by Lucius Junius Brutus, it provoked a legal revolution. In swift order, the Senate banished all the Tarquins, established a republic, and elected Brutus and Collatinus the first consuls for a one-year term. A brief war ensued. The banished king persuaded the powerful Lars Porsena of Clusium to invade Rome; in the defense Horatius heroically held the Sublician bridge, but the Romans were heavily fined and lost some territory. The Tarquin, however, was never heard of again.

Yet under the Etruscan Tarquins, Rome had grown from a swampy market-place of wooden huts to a city of brick and stone. On the drained swampland rose the Forum; on the Capitoline Hill, a citadel; everywhere, temples to the gods. By 560 B. C. the population was probably about two hundred thousand. From the Etruscans, too, the Romans had acquired much: the arch and vault, superstitions and gladiatorial combats, the lares and penates, the toga, and the *fascis*—rods bound with an ax—which would later become the worldwide symbol of Rome. And with the expulsion of the last Tarquin, the Roman Republic was established, to endure for four hundred and eighty years.

TRIREME

This is a Greek trireme—a galley having three banks of oars. Note that the prow is shaped for ramming; and on deck, running from mast to stern, is a great grappling iron. In an ancient sea fight, the ship captain's first action was to ram an enemy ship or shear off its oars. If he was successful, he then grappled and held the disabled vessel, while his men, armed with spears and swords, swarmed aboard it for the final hand-to-hand battle.

VII. Persia and the Golden Age of Greece

550-336 B. C.

The next two centuries were marked by one of the greatest dramas in all history, the clash between Persia and Greece. This was not just the old story of wars; it was a conflict between opposite ways of life.

In the simplest terms, Persia stood for Eastern despotism, while

Greece represented Western democracy. But there was far more to it. For thousands of years autocratic rulers had been necessary for a high level of civilization. Now, among the Hellenes, self-government was being practiced for the first time. This early popular rule had glaring faults. It was unstable, and democratic rights were enjoyed only by a minority. The unit of government remained the small "polis," the single city with its farmlands and villages and seaport. And these Greek city-states engaged in constant civil wars that kept the country in a state of anarchy. They never united except for a brief period in order to defend their land against the invading Persians, a touch-and-go alliance. By contrast, the Persian Empire under Darius was well organized and orderly and even enlightened, welding together all the old cultures and lands—from the valleys of Egypt and Mesopotamia to the coasts of Palestine and Asia Minor, to the mountains of Elam and the Iranian Plateau—into a vast whole that was the culmination of the "Oriental monarchy."

Yet Persia's mighty host, one of the most gigantic of ancient times, was turned back by relatively small Greek armies. This surprising outcome revealed a dramatic fact: free men could fight better than slaves or mercenaries. Liberty, as a political force, had made a brave beginning in the Mediterranean world.

But the victory of Greece was an even greater turning point for mankind. Now she could develop her own dazzling Hellenic culture: an art and architecture of such perfection that they are still called "classical"; a new kind of literature, the drama in addition to her great epics; the most famous schools of philosophy in history; the beginnings of modern science. Most astonishing, these advances were largely concentrated in the city of Athens, in the period following the repulse of the Persians. Herein lay the real Greek victory. Soldiers and ships and courage had merely routed the Oriental invaders. But now the Greeks were shaping a fresh Occidental way of thought. This "Greek way" had a clarity, a light of reason that was the antithesis of the mystery and magic, the god-kings and priests, the despotic order and the social

conservatism of the ancient East. Even the Greek political experiments
(and, alas, their anarchy) were the work of inquiring minds that were
probing for the first time into the nature of the universe, of harmony
and beauty, of man himself. Essentially the triumph of Greece released
her creative energies in a new pattern that would deeply affect the
entire future of civilization.

THE VAST PERSIAN EMPIRE

Cyrus the Great established the Persian Empire, and he truly deserved
the epithet "great."

As a vassal prince of the Medes, he had left his capital and fire-
altar in the Zagros Mountains to seize the throne at Ecbatana. Thereafter he ruled for twenty-one years, adding to his domains, suppressing
revolts, guarding his borders against barbarians, and humanely administering a vast territory.

Conquest, of course, came first. After organizing the Median
Empire and adding it to his own, Cyrus led his army of Medes and
Persians across the Tigris and Euphrates and advanced to the Halys
River, beyond which lay the rich prize of Lydia. The "gilded" Kingdom
of Lydia, embracing the land of the Ionian Greeks, was ruled by
Croesus from his fortified capital of Sardis. This fabulously rich mon-
arch (his name has become a symbol of wealth) was the first to mint
gold coins; in fact, coinage had been invented by the Lydians and
Ionians and then taken up on the Greek mainland. And from Ionia and
the nearby islands had come the first Greek industries and the earliest
flowering of Greek literature and philosophy and science: the poems of
Anacreon and Sappho, Thales' study of nature, the mathematical work
of Pythagoras. Ties of culture and commerce, as well as blood, linked
Greece and Lydia. So now, faced with Cyrus' invading army, Croesus
sought the advice of the Delphic oracle and made an alliance with
warlike Sparta; then he awaited the Persians confidently. But the
Spartans failed to arrive, and Cyrus routed Croesus' army with an

ingenious stratagem. He placed his camels in the forefront of his troops, so that as soon as the Lydian cavalry charged, the horses were terrified by the foul odor of these strange beasts and fled in panic! Sardis was taken, and Croesus himself was about to be executed on a funeral pyre. But he was saved at the last moment, so the story goes, by a sudden thunderstorm sent by Apollo, and by the compassion of the Persian conqueror.

For Cyrus was the first ruler of ancient times to introduce mercy into warfare. Having conquered Lydia, where the remaining Ionian cities were subdued by force or gold, his army swept eastward to the Jaxartes River, then back to Babylon. After a brief fight, the royal family was in Cyrus's hands. Once again he spared a city and a captured king, and even paid his respects to the god Marduk. Then, in a famous act of clemency, he gave freedom to the captive Jews and decreed that they might return to Jerusalem.

This remnant was all that remained of the Hebrews. Thousands of them, taken as roped prisoners to Ashur after the ravaging of Israel, had been scattered in the destruction of Assyria; they were dead or serving new masters. Jerusalem had been an Assyrian vassal for a while and then fallen to Nebuchadnezzar in 586 B. C., when he defeated Pharaoh Necho II for mastery of the coastal states. The Babylonian carried off ten thousand Jewish captives as slaves, and placed Zedekiah on the throne of Judah. But when that unfortunate monarch revolted, Nebuchadnezzar destroyed the city and Solomon's temple and led the remaining inhabitants into captivity. Zedekiah, blinded and bound with fetters of brass, ended his days in a dungeon.

Among the first decrees issued by Cyrus the Great as King of Babylon was the one liberating the Jews. He also ordered the sacred vessels of the temple to be returned. And in 538 B. C., after fifty years of captivity, forty thousand Hebrews left Babylon to return to their homeland. Difficulties beset them, but the Persian officials were helpful, and after twenty-two years of hard work the temple was restored. But captivity had changed the Hebrews. Now they were a theocratic rather than a military nation: they had begun that intense religious and intellectual activity that would produce the world's greatest book, the Bible.

During his remaining years Cyrus received the surrender of Syria, and of Phoenicia with her powerful fleet; he also divided his land into satrapies under satraps or governors. But, unhappily, this magnanimous and humane ruler was succeeded by his ignoble oldest son, Cambyses.

Perhaps Cambyses' reason was affected by the terrible events that began his reign. A brother, Bardiya, attempted to seize the throne and was found stabbed to death on a palace floor. Cambyses had been included in his father's plan to conquer Egypt, and in this he was successful. According to tradition, after conquering Memphis and the Egyptian delta, Cambyses, with an army of fifty thousand men, started across the Libyan desert to capture the rich shrine of Amon in the Oasis of Ammon. A terrible sandstorm overwhelmed them, and only Cambyses, with a few of his captains, returned to the Nile. Thereafter, though his early manner had been benevolent like his father's, the new Persian king became a despot of insane cruelty. He mocked Egypt's religion, murdered priests, committed sacrileges, and slaughtered the population like a veritable madman. In the midst of this horror came news that a magician resembling the dead prince had proclaimed himself king; history knows him as the "false Bardiya." Cambyses hurried home, but died on the way.

But now the empire was fortunate: Darius, satrap of Parthia, was duly chosen king. All the provinces had staged revolts, and there were pretenders to the throne—in addition to the magician—on every side. Darius spent two years putting them down. Then he recorded his victories on a remarkable monument: an inscribed bas-relief, twenty-five feet high and fifty feet wide, situated three hundred and forty feet up a cliff at Behiston in Media! Transcribed between 1835 and 1847 by Sir Henry Rawlinson, the inscription proved to be a trilingual in Old Persian, Babylonian, and Elamite. Like the Rosetta Stone for Egypt, this was the key to the cuneiform tablets of western Asia. And the

DARIUS

In a perfumed palace at Persepolis, Darius the Great receives a deputation of Syrians bringing rich gifts, to renew their allegiance. The king sits on a throne chair; Xerxes, his son and heir, stands beside him; and two guards wait to escort the envoys from the palace after the ceremony.

carved figures show the early triumphs of Darius: he is pictured with his foot resting on the dead body of the false Bardiya, while before him walk eight other defeated claimants, roped neck to neck, their wrists bound together—and a roped Scythian king, captured at the last moment, has been added in front of them. Above the mighty Darius, the god Ahuramazda is seen.

With true administrative genius, Darius reorganized the empire completely. Deciding that henceforth the royal governors must be strictly controlled, he set up the satrapies on a new basis. Three officers were to rule: the satrap (with his secretary), a general, and a tax collector; and they were to be watched by royal inspectors who went from satrapy to satrapy, examining records and seeing that justice and honesty prevailed. These were the famous "eyes and ears of the king."

IT IS THE AGE OF THE PERSIANS

On these facing pages we glimpse part of a long caravan of men,
donkeys, and camels moving slowly over the Plains of Babylon. At
this time, Bactrian camels were used throughout the East as beasts
of burden. Caravans no longer wound along narrow trails, but used
roads built by the Persian kings. Even today, when cars and airplanes
roar across these ancient lands, patient camels plod on the dusty highways. But the camel is a stupid creature, and a bright donkey always
leads the caravan.

His public works, too, were fabulous. Hitherto the roads of Asia
Minor and Mesopotamia had been mere trails on which a caravan could
go single file. Now Darius connected his cities with a network of highways wide enough for chariots. One road between Susa and Sardis was
one thousand six hundred and seventy-seven miles long! Along it were
a hundred and eleven stations where relays of fresh horses were kept

CARAVAN

Earlier we have shown a caravan of Sumer-Akkad. Here is another caravan, two thousand years later. The Bactrian camel has become a beast of burden, and the donkey still holds his place. Thanks to Darius the Great, a caravan can now cross the empire on fine roads and under safer conditions. There are many more caravans than in Sargon's time, and the population has grown; new lands have been occupied. All of Asia Minor—even the Iranian Plateau, and the shores of the Black Sea, where Greeks have settled—is now inhabited by civilized people.

for royal couriers. In times of war or revolution, chariots, carts, cavalry, even foot soldiers could move swiftly on these great roads; in peacetime caravans of donkeys and camels traveled faster and in greater safety.

Waterways too were improved. Negligence and time had filled up the ancient canal of Pharaoh Amenemhet I. Darius had it dredged so that ships could again sail from the Mediterranean up the Nile and through the canal to the Red Sea. Also he had a fleet constructed on the Indus River. Under command of an Ionian Greek named Scylax, these ships sailed downstream into the Indian Ocean, around Arabia to the Red Sea, and then northwest to Egypt—a military and political voyage of exploration that took two and a half years.

And, of course, Darius was a great builder of cities. He started with Susa, which had lain in ruins since its destruction by Ashurbanipal the Assyrian. Here he made a great Persian-style terrace, and on it he erected palaces, government offices, a treasury, and a harem for his

PERSEPOLIS

Here Syrian subjects are bearing gifts to Darius, the Persian king of kings. Directed by court functionaries, they are going up the marble steps that lead to the king's palace, built on the great terrace of Persepolis. Another group is shown, also with gifts—including a Bactrian camel—awaiting its turn.

wives. A contemporary record tells us that he used timber from Gandara and Carmania; gold from Sardis and Bactria; lapis-lazuli and carnelian from Sogdiana; turquoise from Chorasmia; silver and ebony from Egypt; wall ornamentation from Ionia; ivory from Ethiopia, Sind, and Arachosia. And the artisans who cut stone columns, wrought gold, worked wood, baked brick, and decorated walls, included Ionians, Sardians, Medes, Babylonians, and Egyptians.

Perhaps even more beautiful was Darius's new capital, Persepolis, a few miles south of the old seat of Pasargadae. Against a mountainside his workmen constructed a great stone terrace, fifteen hundred feet long and a thousand feet wide. Varying in height from twenty to thirty feet, and protected by fortified walls, this vast terrace was reached by an imposing stairway with a double turn at each side. Facing this, another flight of steps led to the Gate of Xerxes, guarded by sculptured animals. And to the right was Darius's great palace with its seventy-two columns, each sixty-four feet high and capped by sculptured bulls and lion-heads.

Over this vast empire, with its cities and roads and satrapies, shone the benevolent light of the Persian sun-god, Ahuramazda. Originally Medes and Persians worshiped the sun before open-air altars where the sacred fire burned. But the prophet Zoroaster reformed this primitive sun-worship into a faith of good thoughts, good words, good deeds—in which a man must choose between the good lord of light, Ahuramazda, and the wicked lord of darkness, Ahriman. Blood sacrifices were forbidden, intoxicating drinks were banned, believers were required to be kind to animals, to feed the poor, and to protect the weak.

"THE GLORY THAT WAS GREECE"

War between Persians and Greeks was inevitable. Darius was master of all the Near East, save for small belligerent Greece on his left flank. And when the Ionians of Asia Minor rebelled futilely in 499 B. C., Athens had sent a fleet to help them. So the Hellenes had to be conquered.

In 490 B. C. the Persian army sailed across the Aegean, seized an island near Attica, and then—advised by the aged Greek traitor Hippias—swarmed onto the Plain of Marathon near Athens. But on that famous battlefield an Athenian army of perhaps ten thousand, under the command of Miltiades, routed a Persian landing army of maybe three times that number! The massed spearmen of Athens resolutely broke through the line of Persian archers and sent them in headlong flight to their ships. Then the invading fleet went round to the Athenian port of Piraeus, found the victorious army waiting in battle array, and hastily sailed off. The first Persian invasion of Greece was ended.

The second was to be on a much vaster scale. The wise statesman Themistocles persuaded the Athenians to build a great navy, a hundred and eight triremes strong. But Darius was organizing a tremendous army of perhaps a half-million men—the Greek historian Herodotus exaggerated the number to two million six hundred and forty-two thousand. Persians, Medes, Babylonians, Assyrians, Syrians, and all the subject nations contributed—some unwillingly—to this polyglot force. Darius himself died during the preparations. But his son and successor, Xerxes, continued the task and ten years after Marathon led the gigantic army across the Hellespont into Macedonia. It took them seven days to cross from Asia to Europe over a pontoon bridge; a fleet of six hundred and fifty Phoenician-built ships sailed alongside, carrying supplies; and the streams of horsemen, spearmen, archers, charioteers, camp-followers, slaves, and hodge-podge stretched for miles along the paths of Thessaly.

Southward they streamed, stopped only briefly by the heroic defense of Thermopylae in Locris. There a small Greek army under King Leonidas of Sparta held a narrow pass between high cliffs and the sea, till a traitor showed the enemy a back route. Completely surrounded, Leonidas and three hundred Spartans gave their lives in an immortal last stand—but the Persian tide rolled on.

Reaching Athens, the invaders put the deserted city to the torch. The Greek army had withdrawn to the Isthmus of Corinth, but the fleet

THERMOPYLAE

Attacked front and rear, the last of the entrapped Spartans are making
their final stand on the narrow road that runs between a high cliff and
the Aegean Sea at Locris. Of the immortal three hundred dedicated-
to-the-death warriors who faced the Persian host that famous day at
Thermopylae, all were dead by nightfall.

waited nearby at the Bay of Salamis. And there Themistocles tricked
the Persians into attacking. As smoke from Athens rose against the
purple mountains of Attica, Xerxes and his court sat on the heights to
watch the battle. But in the narrow straits, the small, swift Greek
triremes rammed his ships, sheared off their oars, used grappling irons to
board them, sank them one by one. At sundown the Persian fleet was
destroyed, its unlucky seamen drowning in the red waters of Salamis.
Now the disorderly mob that had been the great Persian army dragged

THE PERSIANS RETREAT

Here the defeated Persian host is making its way through a forest in northern Greece, hoping to reach the Hellespont and gain safety in Asia Minor. Xerxes, with his guards, has already reached Sardis and will soon be fleeing along the road that Cyrus built between Sardis and Susa. Xerxes is through with war!

itself back through the mountains of Attica, Boeotia, Locris, Thessaly, Macedonia, and Thrace, unable to find food in the land they had devastated. Thousands died of hunger and disease as the defeated horde streamed back toward Asia. A rear guard, left wintering in Thessaly to cover the retreat, met the same fate in the spring: defeat and massacre by the united Greeks at Plataea, and flight across the Hellespont. The great invasion was over. Never again would a Persian army touch the soil of Greece.

Following the defeat of the Persians, the Athenians rebuilt their burned city and entered an era of magnificence. Politically Athens soon attained power as head of the Delian League, a defensive alliance of the Ionian cities of Asia Minor and the Aegean islands. Athens commanded the joint fleet; then she took the joint treasure that had been kept on the island of Delos, and the League became not a federation but an empire ruled by force. All this came to pass under the greatest of Athenian statesmen, Pericles. First chosen *strategus*, or military leader, in 461 B. C., he was re-elected again and again for thirty-one years. And Athens reached her greatest intellectual and artistic splendor in the Age of Pericles.

A patron of art, philosophy, science, and literature, a friend of genius, Pericles built a splendid monument to Athenian culture: the sacred precinct on the high rocky hill of the Acropolis. Here stood new

GREECE

SCALE OF MILES
0   25   50   75   100

ROUTE OF DARIUS' FLEET 490 B.C. ••••••
ROUTE OF XERXES' ARMY 480 B.C. ———
ROUTE OF XERXES' FLEET 480 B.C. ———

temples of painted marble, the Parthenon with its "perfect" columns, the Theseum, the Erechtheum, the tiny shrine of Nike housing the image of the wingless victory, and the gigantic bronze statue of Athena that could be seen from afar. The buildings were from plans of the architects Ictinus and Callicrates; the sculpture was by Phidias and

others, in marble, bronze, ivory, and gold; the frescoes were painted by
Polygnotus. This was the religious center of the city, dedicated to
Poseidon, god of the sea, and Athena, protectress of wisdom and the
arts. And here, every four years, came the climax of the Great Panathe-
naea festival—the procession winding up through the monumental
gate, bearing a new robe for the goddess.

Over against the cliffs of the Acropolis stood the open-air theater
where Athenians gathered for their favorite entertainment: the twenty-
one plays put on each year as civic undertakings during the Dionysian
festivals. By this time the ancient feasts of singing and dancing and
revelry had given rise to real plays, both tragedy and comedy. Here,
the drama was born. Tragic themes were taken from the myths of
Hesiod and the epics of Homer, but were now represented by masked
and costumed actors and a chanting chorus. Of the many who wrote
tragedies in that era, three are accounted immortal; they spanned the
decades before and after the Age of Pericles. First came Aeschylus,
"father of tragedy," with his stirring pieces about heroic figures doomed
by implacable Fate. Most popular was Pericles' contemporary,
Sophocles, the master of stagecraft and climax and striking characters.
(His *Oedipus the King* remains among the notable plays of the modern
theater.) But most touching was Euripides, whose *Trojan Women* can
still move us to tears over the human suffering and the horrors of war.
In comedy, one name was pre-eminent, Aristophanes, whose plays are
hits today. Comic subjects, unlike tragic ones, were chosen from the
life of the times; and he has left us merciless satires of Athenian politicians, merchants, slaves, generals, and even of Socrates and the new
Sophist philosophers.

For Athens in her prime became the homeland of philosophy—
philosophia, or "love of wisdom." Pericles himself had studied with
Anaxagoras from Ionia, nicknamed "The Mind." And now the learned
men of all Greece walked and taught on these streets, in the great
public marketplace, at the gymnasiums where citizens went in the
afternoons. This was a new kind of education. On a street corner might

be found Zeno, "the philosopher of the two-edged tongue," or Herodotus, the "founder of history." Scientists expounded theories of the universe, Protagoras held forth on ethics and moral law. Everywhere swarmed the Sophists, who claimed to develop the personality—giving instruction in grammar, logic, rhetoric, arithmetic, geometry, music, and astronomy, afterward known as the Seven Liberal Arts. And here in person walked the target of Aristophanes' *The Clouds:* snub-nosed Socrates, prodding men to think for themselves, perhaps the most provocative teacher the world has ever known.

This Athenian cult of beauty and wisdom extended to all Greece and the Greek colonies. Temples were built everywhere (except in Sparta); art was encouraged and learning supported. And to Athens herself, in the time of Pericles, flocked men from every Grecian city and foreign land. Only a small portion of this "glory that was Greece" has survived. But the precious fragments we have, and the influence of this culture on the Mediterranean world, tell us that this was Greece's true Golden Age.

So Athens was indeed as Pericles had said, the "school of Hellas." And all her artistic and intellectual brilliance was truly democratic in character—the amenities were part of the free, public life of the people. Private life, on the other hand, was austere and bare. Contrasting with the magnificence of Acropolis and Agora were narrow, crooked, dirty streets, lined with one- or two-story shops and houses with little distinction—even those of the rich. Each dwelling was built about an open court, where household life centered and into which all rooms opened. There were doors front and back, perhaps a few openings in the outer wall for ventilation, but no chimneys. Smoke from braziers went out through a hole in the roof, or swirled into the court or through an open door. Furnishings were simple—chairs, tables, beds, cooking utensils, a curtain hanging here and there, and gaily decorated pottery oil-lamps to relieve the dullness. Indeed, Pericles' policies were perhaps designed to counteract this barrenness and the poverty that continued to plague Athens even at her height. His building projects gave work

SOCRATES

Here on the mean streets of Athens—in the distance you can see the
Acropolis, crowned by the Parthenon—a Greek philosopher talks to
some young men about truth and virtue and the good life. He teaches
simply, with questions and answers. Yet at the age of seventy this man
was charged by the Assembly with impiety and with corrupting youth.
Tried, found guilty, and condemned to die by his own hand, he chose
to drink hemlock. He was the great Socrates.

to the unemployed; the theater was a means of adult education; the
Sophists sought to prepare the people for the tasks of self-government.

But we need not falsely idealize this Athenian democracy, for two
large groups were deprived of its benefits. Perhaps a third of the population were slaves, though of these the domestic servants and craft
workers were well and even affectionately treated (only the unfortu-
nates in the silver mines at Laurium were worked to death). And the
public and intellectual life of the city was *for men only*—women were

considered inferior beings, confined to the house, legally treated as minors for life. Unattended ladies stayed away from the streets and the market, and only improper females might enjoy the conversation of philosophers!

So Athenian democracy had its seamy side. And the relations between the Greek city-states were tragic. The Age of Pericles was marred by two prolonged wars between Athens and Sparta, that military community under the stern ancient Laws of Lycurgus, where warrior aristocrats still ruled the helots or serfs with an iron hand and looked down on art, literature, luxury, and trade. These Peloponnesian Wars dragged on for decades, and other and worse fratricidal struggles followed, with Persian gold pitting one Greek city against another. Athens shocked all Greece with her enslavement of the rebellious Mytileneans. Then she came under the spell of the charming and dissolute Alcibiades and embarked on a disastrous expedition against the Greek city of Syracuse on the island of Sicily. Her fleet lost and her soldiers slaughtered, prostrate Athens never recovered; in 404 B. C. she fell at last to the Spartan King Lysander. For a time Sparta ruled Greece: aristocrats governed in every community, supported by brutal Lacedaemonian garrisons; while Sparta's ally Persia held Ionia under the infamous "King's Peace." Finally Thebes rebelled; her great general Epaminondas destroyed the Spartan army, and Athens briefly revived the Delian League.

This was the sorry tale of Hellas. In the fifth century B. C. she had attained a brilliance such as the world had never known, a learning and architecture and love of freedom that would inspire mankind for ages. But the "glory that was Greece" went down in treason and mob-rule and shameful civil wars.

The other ancient land that tried self-government, the Roman Republic, took a far different course. To be sure, Rome had factions too, as Athens did: patricians against plebeians, rich against poor, with agrarian laws the focal point. Originally only the patrician Senate of three hundred, meeting in the Forum, could declare war and make peace, vote and rescind laws, and appoint officials (notably the two consuls). In time the rival Assembly of plebeians won the right to name tribunes who could veto the Senate proceedings and even pass the laws.

But where Greeks were quarrelsome and capricious, Romans were stable and the very embodiment of patriotism. Courage, devotion to duty, hard work—those were the "virtues" of the early Romans, whether they were farmers or soldiers. And every Roman was both, from the lowly tiller of the soil to Cincinnatus, summoned from his plow to lead the army. Each able male was a trained, drilled, disciplined, completely loyal soldier, on call from the age of sixteen to sixty. For Rome developed the science of warfare more than any nation since Assyria had done, and Italy was her hard training-ground. The first two centuries of the Republic had to be spent in constant battles with her neighbors. In turn, Rome defeated the Sabines, the Volscians, the Etruscans. Next she bought off a horde of barbarian Gauls and persuaded them to settle in the Po Valley. And finally she completely subdued the other members of the Latin League, becoming the mistress of all Latium. Even so, Rome had still to fight her way to dominance of the Italian peninsula and the western Mediterranean. But already, to the east, both Greece and Persia were breaking down—preparing their own fall to the most famous conqueror in history, Alexander of Macedon.

ALEXANDER AND BUCEPHALUS

Here young Alexander rides Bucephalus—a horse no one else was able to master—before his admiring father, King Philip, and his Macedonian warriors. On Alexander's march into Asia, Bucephalus was never used in battle. In the eastern Iranian Plateau, Alexander built and named a city Bucephala.

VIII.   Alexander the Great

336-323 B. C.

Alexander of Macedon lived the romantic epic of ancient times: in thirteen years this youth conquered most of the old decaying Mediterranean world! But, more important, he changed the very course of civilization.

For his short violent life was dominated by an ideal, *homonoia* or world unity. Originally, the goal was simply Pan-hellenism, or Greek unity; and he acquired it from his tutor, the philosopher Aristotle, but more especially from his father, the warrior King Philip who throve on the tragedy of Hellas.

Greece had been disintegrating for a century when she was brutally united by Philip II of Macedonia. During the endless civil wars, the poor grew more wretched and the rich more frightened, hungry peasants abandoned their devastated farms, unemployed throngs filled the cities, and militarily the land became weaker and weaker. At last she was a ready prey for the Macedonian. Philip had learned the art of war under the Theban Epaminondas; now he trained his own army in a new system of military tactics, a cavalry attack and defense by the "Macedonian phalanx." And then he began his campaign to rule the warring Hellenes. First he extended his boundaries, north in Thrace and east along the Aegean. But when he turned south, he met enraged opposition. Demosthenes, the great orator and demagogue, was thundering his "Philippics" to the Athenian mob; soon every Greek city, except Sparta, declared war. One great battle was fought at Chaeronea in 338 B. C.: Philip routed the allies and found himself master of all Greece.

Next the Macedonian looked to the east and dreamed of attacking Persia. For that vast empire had been crumbling even longer. After his repulse by the Greeks in 480 B. C., Xerxes had withdrawn to Persepolis where he was murdered by eunuchs in his famous Hall of a Hundred Columns. Impotent rulers followed; and one by one the satrapies revolted. The rebellions were put down, but in time much of the fighting was done by Greek mercenaries. Among these were the famous "ten thousand" engaged by the pretender, Cyrus the Younger; when he was killed, they fought their way northward in the dead of winter, until they reached safety at the Black Sea. Their leader, Xenophon, related this "upward march" in his *Anabasis,* and the feat heartened all Hellas. For the next fifty years the Athenian pamphleteer Isocrates vainly urged the Greeks to unite for a mighty assault on Persia, addressing his plan to the Second Athenian League, the kings of Sparta, the tyrants of Cyprus. But finally Philip of Macedon embraced the scheme. He organized a Panhellenic League and had begun to raise forces for the great invasion, when suddenly he was assassinated, probably by an agent of

ALEXANDER AND PHILIP

Here is pictured the famous quarrel between the impetuous Alexander
and his father King Philip of Macedon, on the occasion of Philip's
second wedding. Alexander has just thrown a goblet of wine in the
face of Attalus, the new royal father-in-law. The angry ruler is advancing toward his son with drawn sword. Blood was about to be
shed when Philip stumbled and fell to the floor, too drunk to rise. In
the left background you can see Olympias, Alexander's mother, with
her hand pressed to her cheek. On her right are Attalus and the new
bride.

his wife Olympias, ambitious for her son Alexander. And in 336 B. C.
Alexander himself seized the throne; though only twenty, he was already schooled in statecraft and warfare, and more than prepared to
carry out his father's grandiose plan.

For this young man was also the pupil of Aristotle, greatest philosopher of the age and most universal mind to come out of fourth-century
Athens. That "school of Hellas" was more brilliant than ever in these
dark times; as she and other Greek cities plunged into frenzied political

breakdown, her sages, historians, artists, and scientists drew together into a spiritual union transcending the terror. Socrates had been put to death for subversion in 399 B. C., but his disciple Plato continued to teach for decades in the groves of the Academy, and to write sublime dialogues on love, justice, and the ideal state. And Plato's student Aristotle organized the first systematic collection of human knowledge. As director of the Lyceum, Aristotle supervised the assembly and analysis of all the Greek constitutions, the study and classification of plants and animals. And his own encyclopedic treatises covered logic, metaphysics, physics, astronomy, biology, rhetoric, poetry, ethics, and politics—a vast synthesis that truly expressed Greek cultural unity. This was "The Philosopher," who had been brought to Macedonia to tutor the teen-age heir for seven years.

So when Alexander became king, the entire Panhellenic vision—cultural as well as military—was already his. It was to gain world dimensions in the course of his fantastic career.

A NEW ACHILLES CONQUERS THE WORLD

Young Alexander was truly a royal figure. Superbly handsome and athletic, he was a noble horseman and an inspiring commander, brave to the point of rashness. His mind had been fired by the feats of legendary heroes—he slept with a copy of Homer's *Iliad* by his bed, and believed himself the descendant of the demigods Heracles and Achilles. And he ascended the throne with a sense of mission: he was a "new Achilles" to lead a new war against Asia!

But to the hostile Greeks he was only a beardless boy. So when he tried his strength by raiding north of the Danube, the rumor spread throughout Greece that he had been killed in Illyria. Thebes at once revolted, but Alexander and his army quickly appeared before her walls. The city was taken and looted, and all her buildings razed, except the house where the poet Pindar had lived. Following the destruction of Thebes, all the other Greek cities except Sparta formed a league,

accepted Alexander as their leader, and sent soldiers to join the Macedonian army for the projected Asian invasion. Meantime, Alexander
had made his mother, Olympias, ruler of Macedonia; her first act was
to arrange for the murder of Philip's second wife and child. Olympias
seems to have been deranged, and she ruled badly; the taint would
later appear in her famous son.

But now it was a brilliant young Alexander who marched to war in
Asia with an army of thirty thousand heavily armed troops. They were
Macedonians, Thracians, Greeks, and Cretans, besides five thousand
regular Macedonian cavalry. With them they also took siege towers and
machines. In addition, Alexander had an elite body of aristocratic Macedonian horsemen, eight cavalry squadrons of two hundred and fifty men
each. The first "royal" squadron was led by Alexander himself, with
"Black" Cleitus second in command. Accompanying the army went a
group of historians, architects, poets, doctors, and scientists, who were
to observe and collect records and specimens for Aristotle, Alexander's
old teacher.

After crossing the Hellespont to Troad, the army camped on the
plain before the site of ancient Troy. There Alexander paid his homage
to the heroic dead, and prayed that he might be worthy of his illustrious
lineage.

From Troy, Alexander's army marched east to his first great victory.
At the Granicus River the Persian army, reinforced by Greek mercenaries, awaited them. Here, as in all his future battles, the young Alexander
personally led the attack and was always in danger. Charging headlong
against the enemy, he terrified not only his foes but his father's old generals, who could not dissuade him from taking needless risks. Under his
leadership, the battle was soon over. The Persian-Greek force broke,
unable to stand against the phalanx, and was speedily cut to pieces by
the Macedonian cavalry. Such was the historic Battle of Granicus, 334
B. C.—apparently it showed Alexander his destiny. For now he decided
on the epic conquest of all Persia, to bring Greek civilization to the
entire Oriental world!

ALEXANDER THE GREAT

Alexander of Macedon, the most romantic warrior in history, is shown here charging the Persians at Issus. He was a great leader, a skilled fighter, and brave beyond measure—often to the dismay of his own army. Though he risked his life a thousand times in war, legend has it that he died in bed of a fever at the age of thirty-three, in the Babylonian palace of Nebuchadnezzar. His sprawling empire was left to his quarreling captains.

First, however, he fulfilled an old Panhellenic ambition: he marched south along the Aegean, freeing the Ionian cities from Persian rule. The mighty Phoenician fleet, allied to Persia, still dominated the Aegean waters. But Alexander's Macedonian garrisons and his regent Antipater controlled the volatile Ionians and prevented them from being incited to revolt by the Phoenicians. And the youthful king himself spent the winter in campaigns against the hill tribes of Pisidia.

But now the Macedonian army marched toward the heart of the great Persian Empire of forty million souls. On they went, through

a difficult mountain pass called the Cilician Gates, and around the
northeast corner of the Mediterranean—when suddenly news came that
Darius's forces had crossed into Cilicia and were at their rear. Alexander
turned quickly and met the Persians in a great battle on the shores of
the Gulf of Issus. This was the main Persian army: one hundred and
fifty thousand men, including fifteen thousand Greek mercenaries, all
under the personal command of Darius III. But again Alexander's tactics prevailed. The Persian center and left broke before the phalanx,
and the Macedonian horsemen savagely destroyed them. Convinced
that the day was lost, Darius fled the field in his chariot, leaving his
wife, mother and two daughters to be taken captive.

Thus the King of Persia escaped, and soon sent Alexander a
lavish peace offer—Darius would surrender all Asia west of the Euphrates! Philip's old general, Parmenio, urged acceptance; with the prof-
ferred territory, Macedonians and Greeks would be forever safe from
Asiatic invasion. But the young conqueror retorted with spirit: Were he
Parmenio, he would accept; being Alexander, he must say no. In
truth he could not rest till he had crushed Persia completely, by land
and sea.

So now Alexander struck at Persia's sea power. Turning to the
Mediterranean coast, he advanced on the great Phoenician ports. Sidon
gave up peacefully, but Tyre, built on an island, resolved to fight behind its massive walls. After throwing a causeway over from the mainland, Alexander marched his men across it with siege-engines and
towers and invested the city. For seven months the Tyrians held out;
then the walls weakened and the city was taken by assault. As a punishment for resisting, eight thousand men of Tyre were killed and thirty
thousand enslaved. After that, Damascus and Jerusalem surrendered
quickly. The Philistine stronghold of Gaza blocked the advance, but
every man was killed and the city razed. Soon all the coastal cities were
captured and destroyed. And the great Phoenician fleet—with no port
where it could repair or replenish its vessels—was scattered and destroyed without a fight. Some ships were sunk by storms, some beached

on far shores, and a few perhaps reached safety in the African city of Carthage.

Fresh from the conquest of the coastal states, Alexander and his army now crossed the Sinai Desert and entered the ancient land of Egypt. Here they were greeted as friends who had come to free the Nile Valley from two centuries of Persian despotism. Alas, Egypt was not to be free. For four hundred years she had been overrun by foreigners— Ethiopians, Assyrians, Babylonians, Persians—and now it was the Macedonians and Greeks. And for the next three hundred years she was to be ruled by the Greek Ptolemies.

But in a curious way Egypt managed to enslave her conqueror, Alexander the Great. From boyhood on he had been very religious, with an apparently irrational mysticism. And in his youth Olympias had hinted to him that his father was not Philip but a god! Now, deeply impressed by the great Egyptian temples and their mysterious old rites, he decided to consult a famous shrine of Amon-Ra (who corresponded to the Greek Zeus), in the remote oasis of Siwa. There a pliant high priest, used to semidivine Egyptian pharaohs, obligingly questioned the oracle —which naturally proclaimed Alexander a son of Zeus-Amon. With perhaps a touch of his mother's madness, Alexander was thoroughly convinced that he was a demigod.

Or was it genius instead? For next Alexander devised a plan for a magnificent Hellenic city—a new port, named Alexandria—to be built in the Nile Delta, with palaces, temples, and planned streets. The details he left to be executed by his architect Dinocrates, but he had chosen the site wisely; his city would supplant ruined Tyre as the greatest seaport of the eastern Mediterranean. It was the first of many Greek-style "Alexandrias" that he would build on strategic trade routes throughout the Near East.

But for the present Alexander was still a warrior, with the Persian heartland to conquer. So he now returned with his army to Tyre, then marched northeast and crossed the Euphrates and Tigris. And finally, on October 1, 331 B. C., he met and annihilated the last Persian army at

THE DEATH OF DARIUS

After the disaster at Guagamela a band of Persians, led by the
Bactrian viceroy Bessus, kidnaped Darius and fled to the mountains
of Media, where they murdered their unhappy king. His body, left in
a rude wagon, was discovered by the pursuing Macedonians. Here
Alexander rides up at dawn to view the remains of Darius III, last of
the Achaemenian line.

Gaugamela. The exact date is known because an eclipse of the moon
had occurred eleven days earlier. And we have precise knowledge of
the famous battle. Darius's new chariots had scythes projecting from
their axles to mow down the enemy, but they failed. The polyglot mob
of the Persian king—archers and spearmen on horse, on foot, in chariots
—fought desperately but hopelessly against the Macedonian phalanx of
shields and spears, and the charge of the Greek cavalry.

With the Battle of Gaugamela won, all Persia now fell into the hands of the twenty-four-year-old Alexander. On his triumphant advance, he paused briefly in the land of Media, to view the remains of Darius III—the defeated Great King had been kidnaped and then murdered by his own officers.

Next Alexander received the submission of Babylon, plundered that city, and passed on to Susa, where he was welcomed as a liberator. There, in the vaults of Darius, he found a treasure of fifty thousand talents—three hundred thousand dollars! But the tomb of Cyrus the Great, which he visited later, had long since been robbed and he found only the withered body of greatness on the dusty floor. For two hundred years had passed since the Persian nomads, with Cyrus at their head, marched victorious through the land of the Two Rivers. And now it was the new conqueror, Alexander the Great, who advanced in state to the magnificent city of Persepolis, capital of Persia.

THE EAST CONQUERS THE DEMIGOD

But from then on the epic of Alexander entered a new phase: the "mysterious East" gradually took possession of its Hellenic conqueror. At times he exhibited a breathtaking world vision and geographic grasp; he was a humane emperor, seeking a new fusion of East and West. Then again he indulged in cruelty and luxury and debauchery, like a corrupt Oriental potentate.

Thus, while he was still at Persepolis, Alexander threw a torch during a drunken brawl and set fire to the royal palace. Plutarch, the Greek historian, describes the scene vividly: Alexander's feast in the Hall of a Hundred Columns; the Athenian dancer Thais, later the wife of Ptolemy and queen of Egypt, asking leave to burn down the palace of Xerxes who had reduced "fair Athens" to ashes; Alexander and Thais with flaming torches, leading riotous lines of Macedonian revelers through the great halls, setting fire to everything inflammable, till the magnificent building was a mass of flames. The next morning a contrite

Alexander viewed the smoking ruins, but there were to be further disgraceful episodes.

Meantime, however, the conqueror embarked on a fantastic military campaign worthy of Aristotle's pupil—to reduce the little-known frontier territory of eastern Persia and the remote Indus valley. He left his trusted general Parmenio in charge at the Median capital of Ecbatana. There he turned eastward; he led his army almost to the Caspian Sea and into fabulous semibarbaric lands: Parthia, Aria, and Arachosia. In savage guerrilla warfare, they fought their way through wild steppes and harsh deserts, icy mountains and savage torrents. Turning north, into what is now Turkestan, Alexander passed the nomad capital Samarkand. As he went he founded many cities—a line of garrisons and trading posts all through Central Asia—and named each one Alexandria. Finally he turned south, going through the Khyber Pass into India, where he defeated Rajah Porus and a squadron of elephants. Still he pressed on, through tropical heat and monsoon rains, hoping to learn if that fabled country was the end of the earth!

But his ragged, weary troops had had enough of strange geography. Ten thousand had died from thirst, hunger, and fighting; now they mutinied and forced Alexander to turn back. Nonetheless, on the return journey he continued his explorations, dividing his forces into three groups. One contingent was sent northwestward; the fleet, commanded by Nearchus, sailed down to the mouth of the Indus and up the Persian Gulf to the Pasatigris River; and Alexander himself led the main body west from Pittala (Hyderabad), across the desolate sands along the Gulf, and to Persepolis at last. They had been gone six years and had trekked some five thousand miles!

In his capital once more, Alexander found his empire in disorder. The satraps of Bactria and Media were in revolt; Harpacus, the treasurer, had absconded with the royal funds. The situation might have dismayed a lesser man. But the erstwhile conqueror lost no time in setting to rights an empire that now stretched from Greece and Egypt all the way to India.

His statesmanship was as brilliant and exotic as his campaigns, and it too finally cost him the support of his loyal followers. They applauded when he promoted trade and Hellenic culture, introducing an imperial silver currency, deepening rivers and building wharves from the Nile to Mesopotamia to the Indus, encouraging Greek colonization of his new cities and Greek-style festivals and games. But Alexander also played the hated role of an Oriental god-of-empire. Already he had antagonized the Macedonian generals—by appointing Persians to high office, by marrying the Bactrian Princess Roxana, and by training Asiatic soldiers. He even commanded that all must prostrate themselves in his divine presence, but this order was rescinded. Now, however, he sent orders to the Hellenic League that he was to be numbered among the gods of each Greek city. And he decreed a great and symbolic marriage ceremony at Susa in 324 B. C., a festival known to the ancients as the "wedding of Asia and Europe." In one day Alexander married both Statira, daughter of Darius III, and Paysatis, daughter of Artaxerxes III, thereby attaching himself to both royal families of Persia. At the same time eighty of his officers took Persian brides, while on the following day nine thousand of his soldiers married Persian women. (This was revolutionary, for Greek laws punished intermarriage by loss of citizenship.) Each bridegroom received a golden cup and rich presents from the god-emperor Alexander, who drank a toast to *homonoia*, or unity between conquerors and conquered. Plutarch adds that Alexander meant to achieve "unity among all men, and peace" and that he wished "the whole earth to obey one word of command."

That was the climax of Alexander's career: the rest was swift decline. He had only a short time longer to live.

His whole life had been shadowed by the conviction that he would die early, and fateful omens suggested that the time was at hand. Crows fought on the city walls, and a lion was kicked to death by an ass. A soothsayer warned that misfortune awaited him in Babylon. When Apollodorus, the Greek governor of the city, had the liver of a sacrificed sheep examined, the prophecy was "disaster." Alexander himself felt that he had lost the protection of the gods; he consulted purifiers and fortune-tellers, but these only added to his terror of death. His days were indeed numbered, though he would die from his own excesses and not by an assassin's hand.

Yet the doomed emperor still had flashes of genius. From the West he received the ambassadors of Carthage and Italy and Spain, and doubtless talked of "concord"; for the East he organized two naval forces, one to explore the Caspian Sea, and the other, under Nearchus, to circumnavigate Arabia. Then he gave a farewell banquet for the Arabian expedition—it proved to be his own farewell, instead. The next day a fever seized him and he was put to bed. It was the eighteenth day of Daesius (June). A week later the fever reached its height and he became unconscious; and his Macedonian generals and officers, who had kept watch within the court, passed unarmed by his bedside to bid farewell to their great leader. He died at Babylon on the evening of the twenty-eighth of June, 323 B. C., at the age of thirty-three years.

In his brief lifetime he had established the largest empire yet known; after his death, he became a figure of legend in a dozen lands. But what did he really accomplish? Alexander the Great had conquered all the crumbling lands of the eastern Mediterranean, and in so doing had changed the course of history. But the full fruits of that conquest—both good and evil—would ripen only in the succeeding age.

IX. Rise and Fall of the Hellenistic Age

321-146 B. C.

After Alexander's death, what befell his splendid dream of bringing Greek culture to a united world?

The vision of universal empire seemed doomed. When the precocious youth died, his far-flung lands were carved up by his generals. Then they and their successors plunged into an orgy of wars and realignments for the next hundred and fifty years.

But "Hellenism"—a diffused culture of Greek, or Hellenic, origin— became a reality. The new Macedonian monarchs built great cities that became marvels of the age. Alexandria in Egypt was the center of a brilliant new civilization that spread to the farthest corners of the erstwhile Alexandrine Empire. Its influence was felt as far west as Syracuse and Spain and as far east as distant China! Now Greek literature, Greek architecture, and above all the Greek spirit of inquiry spread clear around the Mediterranean: it was an era of scholars, investigators, experimenters, that laid the foundations of modern science and technology.

In all these centers men spoke one simple Greek dialect, the "common tongue"; and astronomers and mathematicians in different countries pooled their knowledge and observations. The known world was linked together by trade as never before, for most Hellenistic rulers continued to use Alexander's coinage based on the Attic standard. Their ships were larger and faster, their mariners had charts with latitude and longitude; while overland, the old Persian roads were extended, and caravan routes were protected by patrols and post stations. So an un-heard-of volume of trade goods poured through the Mediterranean and nearby areas, especially luxuries for all the new capitals. For the first time in history there was an *oikoumene*—a civilized world community.

But in the east, this brilliance was a veneer. The dazzling cities were on the seacoast, the luxury and enlightenment strictly for the upper classes. Underneath, the masses sank deeper into misery, and there were no official attempts to ease their lot—only pathetic revolts by Greek peasants and slaves and serfs, organized "flights" by the patient fellahin of the Nile. For the age carried the seeds of its own destruction: in the terrible battles with charging war-elephants in Asia Minor, in the blind extravagance of the Ptolemies in Egypt, in the brutal Hellenization of the Jews at Jerusalem. Empires crashed against each other constantly, the smaller ones shattering, the larger ones weakening. And gradually, relentlessly, the new Roman power from the west moved in to pick up the pieces.

Yet in its very crumbling—as in its brilliance and sense of one culture—the Hellenistic Age was preparing the way for Alexander's true heir: Rome, the inheritor of Greek civilization and unifier of the ancient world.

HELLENISM IN THE EAST: CHAOS AND SPLENDOR OF THE NEW MONARCHIES

Chaos was Alexander's direct legacy: he left no designated heir and no organization. So when he died there was a bloody scramble for power, during which his mother, his weak-minded half-brother, his widow, and her child all perished. Finally his empire was divided into five parts, each ruled by a Macedonian general. Asia Minor went to Antigonus, Babylon to Seleucus, Thrace to Lysimachus, Greece and Macedonia to Antipater, and Egypt to Ptolemy. These successors, or "Diadochi," pledged oaths of eternal friendship—and at once organized their armies for war.

For a half-century the cataclysmic Wars of the Diadochi raged over the Near East. Large numbers of elephants were used; at Ipsus in Asia Minor, the allied kings of Babylon and Thrace kept a herd of 480. In battle these beasts were goaded into thunderous charges, or their huge bodies were lined up broadside to halt advancing cavalry. Thus the new monarchs fought one another savagely till only two great empires were left—the Seleucid Kingdom to the east of the Mediterranean, and Ptolemaic Egypt. Then these empires too started to crumble as the fighting went on. Meantime Antipater had been harshly putting down rebellious Greeks, and thereafter the Greek peninsula itself was rocked by a final round of devastating civil wars.

Yet, despite the constant warfare, the Diadochi created the Hellenistic world that Alexander had dreamed of. Schools of Hellenic art, poetry, drama, science, and philosophy flourished throughout the Mediterranean, in the new capitals of the warring successors as well as in the older Greek cities. And now Alexandria was the great cultural center, as Athens had been before.

Envisioned by Alexander himself, and carried out by the architect Dinocrates, the great new Egyptian capital of Alexandria was a planned city—a rarity in ancient as in modern times. It was a splendid sight at the mouth of the Nile, with a famous landmark in the harbor, the Pharos lighthouse. This wondrous tower, of white marble decorated with bronze and marble sculpture, rose to a height of perhaps four hundred feet; and its light, from a resinous wood, reflected by metal mirrors, could be seen at a distance of thirty-eight miles! The city proper had streets that crossed each other at right angles, and a broad avenue three miles long bisected Alexandria from east to west. On the main thoroughfare were located the king's palace, the golden sarcophagus of Alexander, and—most famous of all—the intellectual center of the world.

For here was the great "Museum" or home of the Muses: a royal park with white marble temples of learning and tree-shaded porticoes, and its own theater, gymnasium, lecture hall, scientific centers, and observatory. The celebrated group of buildings was no ordinary university but an institute for advanced study and research, a school for scholars.

There were four main groups of these savants—astronomers, mathematicians, physicians, and writers—and they included some of the most learned men of all time. Here Euclid composed his celebrated *Elements*, which is still used as a geometry textbook today. Here Aristarchus advanced the notion that the earth revolved around the sun; and after him, Hipparchus completed celestial observations that would form the basis of Ptolemaic astronomy for more than a millennium. Here Archimedes of Syracuse advanced the science of mechanics and invented his famous "endless screw" for raising water. Geographical knowledge was spurred by Eratosthenes, who calculated the circumference of the earth. In anatomy, Herophilus dissected the corpses of executed criminals, to discover that the heart propelled the blood and the brain was the center of the nervous system. Annexed to the Museum was the Library, the largest ever assembled, with three-quarters of a million books on rolls; it attracted historians, philologists, and literary men, among them the Sicilian pastoral poet Theocritus. Scholars from all over the Mediterranean came to this beautiful park.

Unfortunately, this Alexandrian science, the basis of much later scientific progress, did little for the masses in its own age. It had a practical use in the making of world maps for navigators, and in the new engines of war perfected by Archimedes. But except for rotary corn-mills, almost no labor-saving machines were built; slaves were much too cheap and plentiful. The constant senseless wars of the Hellenistic monarchs had swollen the slave-population of the ancient world; in all their countries save Egypt (which had its own totalitarian set-up), industry and agriculture were operated by slave labor. Even Hellenistic schools of philosophy—stoic, epicurean, cynic—were part of this over-all picture. They were concerned with liberating men's minds and finding man's place in the universe, but in a world in which little could be done about widespread injustice, their practical effect was on individual adherents. Later ages would make social applications of much Hellenistic science. But the mechanical wonders described by Heron—water-clocks, water-organs, automata, and the like—were only rich men's toys or temple tricks to delude the curious. Nevertheless, the Museum and Library did help to make Alexandria the most brilliant city of a peculiarly brilliant time.

And the splendors of Alexandria were repeated, on a lesser scale, in other famous centers of the era. Thus, on the long trade route from the Mediterranean to the Persian Gulf, the Seleucids built two great cities: Seleucia, their eastern capital on the Tigris, and Antioch in Syria. Antioch, the "Queen of the East," reached a population of a half-million and was renowned for its luxury, its sumptuous streets illuminated all night, and its extravagant marble-and-gold statue of Apollo with two large jacinths for eyes! More classical was Pergamum in Asia Minor—the so-called "Athens of Asia"—which ranked for a while as the second city of the Hellenistic world. Rising on a steep hill a thousand feet above the plain, the Pergamene Acropolis had a wealth of colonnaded architecture including a huge gymnasium for the education of boys and girls, and an impressive library where books were copied onto skins of "charta pergamena" (hence our word parchment). But its most famous treasure was the Great Altar of Zeus, whose immense frieze represented the triumph of civilization over barbarism. Another celebrated capital was Rhodes, situated on the Greek island of that name. In the third century B. C. Rhodes, with the bronze Colossus in its harbor, was considered the most beautiful city of Hellas; and it was an important business mart besides, famous for honesty, uprightness, and good faith in a world of commercial trickery. When in 225 B. C. Rhodes suffered a destructive earthquake—the Colossus toppled and the port was ruined—all Greece came to its assistance with money, materials, food, and labor. In addition to these great centers, even small Hellenistic towns had temples and statues and theaters, and of course plenty of slaves.

These cities were noted, too, for their various schools of Hellenistic art. Now movement and violence had invaded the serenity of Periclean sculpture. The fashion was for lively, realistic groups of gods and goddesses; portraits cast from the sitters; exaggerated, heroic reliefs in marble and bronze; genre pieces illustrating daily life. In size these sculptures ranged from the graceful eight-inch terra-cotta figurines of Tanagra, in Greece, to the towering one-hundred-and-five-foot Colossus. Some of the most famous masterpieces of antiquity have survived from this period—the Laocoön, the Dying Gaul, the Apollo Belvedere, the Venus of Milo. And one particular find has been considered the loveliest sculptured figure in the world. Buried deep in the earth on the island of Samos, the Winged Victory of Samothrace was uncovered in 1863. With its beautiful body, flying draperies, and outspread wings, this stone Nike seems to live and move, though it is mutilated and its head and arms are lost. Even so, all these works bore the signs of the age: great technical skill, lifelike imitation of nature, frenzied motion, and exaggeration. Gone was the "golden mean" of classical times; Greece herself did a thriving business copying the prettified statues of Praxiteles!

And administratively the Hellenistic Age was a time of bankruptcy; the brilliant end of a Greek culture imposed by force on subject peoples. In Egypt the Ptolemies had taken over and intensified the ancient autocratic system under which the Pharaoh owned the country. At first Greek bureaucrats and administrators ran the irrigated Nile Valley as a great improved farm, introducing superior seed corn and livestock, iron tools, the Archimedean screw for irrigation. But it was still the peasants—the fellahin—who toiled in the black mud under the hot sky, and delivered half their produce to the royal granaries. Control was now absolute: every craft, every business belonged to the government; everything was ordered and taxed, with a ten-per-cent sales tax topping all the rest. And in time, this led to rampant oppression and extortion—the Rosetta Stone itself was a futile reform decree—and decay spread from top to bottom. Alexandria remained a center of Hellenistic art and learning; but the Ptolemaic court, fascinated by the mystic religion and culture of ancient Egypt, became decadently Egyptian. Courtiers practiced the age-old rituals and worshiped Osiris instead of Zeus, and Isis instead of Hera; and gradually the immense wealth of the Ptolemies and the accompanying luxury corrupted and destroyed them. Ptolemy I had been a king of integrity, and the land had prospered under his son and grandson. But for three centuries their successors grew progressively weaker. All Egypt's territories were gradually lost—Cyrene, Cyprus, and possessions around the Aegean–till only the Nile Valley was left. And there the deterioration continued. The Egyptian people, untouched by the Hellenistic brilliance, went their silent sullen way in mounting hatred of their Greek overlords. Half-enslaved Egyptian field hands now began organized "strikes"; in growing numbers they left their work and fled repeatedly to the sanctuary of temples. Of course, soldiers brought them back. But the land lay fallow, irrigation ditches filled with silt— and the palace of the extravagant Ptolemies was smeared with dynastic blood.

The Seleucid Empire too shrank steadily. One by one, her provinces seceded: Armenia, Cappadocia, Pontus, Bactria, and Sogdiana. The province of Persia was captured by barbarians and became Parthia, and a rebellious officer seized a fortified hill in Asia Minor and founded the kingdom of Pergamum. In this disintegration the signs of decadence multiplied. And finally, whereas Hellenization had been only an intellectual veneer in Egypt, in Palestine it became a brutal horror.

During the wars of the Ptolemies and Seleucids, Judea had been a bone of contention, passing from one empire to the other. The earlier rulers, however, continued the beneficent policy of the Persians and Alexander and respected the religious fervor of the Jews. For by now Hebrew scholars and scribes had given final form to the books of the Old Testament: the inspired chronicle of God and His chosen people, with all the commandments and psalms and exhortations of the prophets. And the Holy Bible—its study and the carrying out of the precepts of the Law—had become the main concern of the Israelites, who now considered themselves the "people of the Book."

But under the Seleucid King Antiochus IV a tragic ordeal began for this pious nation. Regarding Judea as simply a source of revenue,

Antiochus raised taxes, sold the office of the high priest to the highest bidder, and introduced into Jerusalem every phase of Greek life that was anathema to the Jews. He did violence to their sacred rites, desecrated the temple, and left nothing undone to destroy their ancient culture. So when Antiochus attempted to invade Egypt in 169 B. C., a rumor that he had been killed set off a great uprising in Jerusalem. Rejoicing, the Jews murdered their brethren who had been Hellenized, cleansed the temple of pagan abominations, and began killing every Greek in sight. But at this juncture Antiochus returned and reduced Jerusalem to a shambles. In revenge he proceeded to despoil the temple and seize all the golden vessels; he restored the hated Menelaus to the position of high priest; he instituted the death penalty for anyone professing the Jewish faith; he outlawed all Jewish rituals. Anyone owning the Book of the Law was considered a traitor, and the holy temple became a shrine for Zeus.

To escape the thousand infamies forced upon them, many Jews fled to the hills. Soon a Jewish priest named Mattathias the Hasmonean, and his five sons—the Maccabees—became the leaders of guerrilla warfare in the mountains. As each member of the family was slain, the next in turn assumed leadership, and gradually the resistance reached triumphant proportions. Under Judas Maccabeus the Jewish forces entered Jerusalem and solemnly rededicated the temple. And under his brother Simon they succeeded in establishing a Second Jewish Commonwealth, ruled by the new Hasmonean dynasty.

But the restored Hebrew kingdom would have only a short independence. Along with the rest of Alexander's shattered empire, Jerusalem was destined to fall to the conquering legions of Rome.

HELLENISM IN THE WEST: ROME ARISING, CARTHAGE FALLING

Even as the empire of the Successors crumbled in the East, Rome was rising in the West—preparing for her own adoption of Hellenistic culture even as she toppled the maritime rule of "Oriental" Carthage.

First, of course, came Rome's bitter battles to conquer the whole of Italy. The very same year that the Diadochi divided the vast Alexandrine Empire, the small Roman nation was losing her second war to the Samnites in the Apennines. At the narrow pass of Caudine Forks most of her army was captured and forced to pass under the "yoke," an arch of Samnite spears. Then the Gauls and Etruscans joined the victorious Samnites in an alliance against Rome. Characteristically, Rome was not discouraged. She organized and trained a new force, and twenty-six years later she defeated the allied armies at Sentinum in 295 B. C. Her triumph was complete. The twelve walled Etruscan cities became, by treaty or force, a part of her state; the land of the Samnites was henceforth her territory; the Gauls were driven north of the Arnus. Below that river, all Italy was Rome's except the Greek settlements in the south, and to these she gave an ultimatum: alliance or war. Three cities became allies, but the largest, Tarentum, chose to fight, with help from Epirus, directly across in Greece. Its king, Pyrrhus, crossed the Ionian Sea to Italy with a well-trained force of twenty-five thousand infantry, three thousand cavalry, and twenty elephants. A brilliant leader, he won a series of victories against the Romans and the Sicilian Carthaginians. But they were "Pyrrhic victories," so costly that they decimated his army. After six years of fighting, King Pyrrhus sailed home in defeat with the remnant of his troops. At last the peninsula was Roman, clear down to the toe of the boot.

And now came the terrible struggle between Rome and Carthage for the mastery of the western Mediterranean. Founded some five hundred years earlier, Carthage had become the center of a great empire. She held the African coast from Cyrene west to the Straits of Gibraltar and into Spain, and her possessions included the islands of Corsica and Sardinia and half of Sicily. Many Libyans now crowded her great port with its population of seven hundred thousand. But essentially her people retained the traits of the first Phoenician settlers: black-bearded Semitic merchants with shaved upper lips, clad in long bright-colored robes and high turbans of striped scarves; fearless barelegged sailors, with earrings and short tunics and flashing knives. For Carthage was always a maritime and commercial center. Her seamen sailed even into the Atlantic, north to Britain for tin, and south for twenty-six hundred miles along the west coast of Africa. And her merchant ships visited all friendly harbors.

By 264 B. C., when the trouble with Rome started, Carthage was the richest capital on the Mediterranean Sea. Along her waterfront stretched vast warehouses and docks where ships loaded and unloaded from daybreak to dusk. Their cargoes included treasures from everywhere on earth: linen and goblets from Egypt, beautifully decorated Greek pottery, gold and ivory from Africa. This was a city of merchant kings, of wealth and splendor, whose whole life was trade. She bought and sold goods made by the whole ancient world.

So her main life centered in the port. But there was also an official center of town, a citadel where impressive temples and government buildings stood. And the landward side of the city was protected by a great wall forty-five feet thick, cut at intervals by high towered gates. Within these gates were arsenals, army barracks, and stables for horses and war elephants. Carthage, with her extensive colonies, was a military as well as a naval power.

Outside the walls of the city were the estates of the wealthy. Here the clever Carthaginians, among the most skillful agriculturalists of their time, irrigated the land and grew grain, vegetables, and fruits. They also raised horses, asses, donkeys, sheep, goats, and cattle, and kept stables of large-eared African elephants. And the scale of this farming was truly prodigious: the Carthaginians perfected the gigantic plantation. On a single estate, the fields might be tilled and the flocks tended by as many as ten thousand slaves.

For Carthage was famous for her prosperous planters, her merchant princes, her treasure-laden fleet. This was the western metropolis founded by the old seafaring Phoenicians—who had brought with them their love of wealth, their skill at trade, and their ancient coarse deities. Chief god was Baal-Hamen, to whom infants were sacrificed;

ROME
IN ITALY

SCALE OF MILES

0   50   100   150

ALPS

RIVER PO

ARNUS R.

RAVENNA

RUBICON R.

ARNUS R.

SENTINUM
295 B.C.

METAURUS
RIVER 207 B.C.

Lake
TRAS-
IMENE
217 B.C.

TIBER R.

VEII

ROME

CAPUA

NAPLES

VESUVIUS

CANNÆ
216 B.C.

APPIAN WAY

BRUNDISIUM

TARENTUM

THURII

LOCRI

MESSINA

ADRIATIC SEA

ILLYRIA

IONIAN
SEA

TYRRHENIAN SEA

ITALY

APENNINES

STRAIT OF

STRAIT OF MESSINA

SICILY

SYRACUSE

CARTHAGE

N
W
E
S

and some other divinities were the fertility goddess Tanith, and Esh-mun, the god of health and wealth. Carthage controlled the rich over-land trade with the interior of Africa and the even richer maritime trade of the western Mediterranean, and this brought her into direct conflict with Rome.

By now Rome was mistress of Italy and could no longer endure Carthaginian restraints on her commerce. The two rivals kept edging closer, till they finally collided over possession of the Sicilian town of Messina. On that pretext, in 264 B. C., the Roman Senate at last de-clared war on Carthage.

Now followed the two "Punic" (or Phoenician) Wars by which Rome broke the might of Carthage in the western Mediterranean. The first conflict lasted more than two decades and marked the emergence of Roman sea-power. While the Carthaginians fought and idled, the Romans met triumph and defeat with equal fortitude, and built up a navy of great quinqueremes, warships with five banks of oars. One Roman victory, off Cape Economus in Sicily in 256 B. C., was the biggest sea battle of ancient times; perhaps 660 vessels and 300,000 men took part. In the end, Carthage was forced to accept a harsh peace. Rome gained all Sicily, plus Sardinia and Corsica, and the old restrictions on her shipping were lifted. Carthage had to pay an immense fine: 450 talents ($1,584,000) each year for ten years, and a further levy of 1200 talents.

But the seeds had been sown for the Second Punic War. At the altar of Baal-Hamen, the Carthaginian general Hamilcar Barca (with his nine-year-old son Hannibal) vowed eternal vengeance. Hamilcar began the task, conquering Spain and there assembling a great invasion force of Numidian, Libyan, and Spanish mercenaries; but he was assas-sinated, as was his son-in-law and successor. At twenty-six, Hannibal became the elected leader of the mercenary army and prepared to carry out the destruction of Rome.

Hannibal nearly succeeded in one of the most spectacular cam-paigns in history. The Romans felt reasonably safe; Carthage was

HANNIBAL'S INVASION OF ROME

Here we see the army of Hannibal, the Carthaginian—it was composed mainly of Nubian and Spanish mercenaries—descending the Alps into Italy, led by enormous African elephants. Hannibal was one of the great generals of all time. For sixteen years, with no aid from his homeland and always outnumbered, he won impossible victories and terrorized Rome, until he was recalled to Carthage, and political defeat.

paying her fine, and the last Gauls had been driven out of Italy. Then Hannibal struck. He marched through Gaul and crossed the Alps in late fall and early winter. Passing crevasses, avoiding avalanches, cutting paths for horsemen and elephants, lashed by snow and sleet, harassed by Alpine tribes, exhausted and hungry, Hannibal finally reached the Po Valley with his army. He had thirty-four thousand warriors to face the might of Rome; six thousand of his men had died in the ice of the Alps. And Rome was raising a tremendous force to meet him with odds of ten to one.

Yet in battle after battle this fabulous commander defeated and destroyed every Roman army he met. At the Ticino River he routed the forces of the Consul Scipio. At Lake Thrasimene he ambushed and slaughtered thirty thousand Romans commanded by the Tribune Flaminius. And at Cannae—one of the classic battles of all time—Hannibal's strategy was a work of art. Facing a force double his own, he selected his field and then set and moved his Numidian cavalry and Spanish and Libyan infantry at just the right moments, like pieces in a gigantic game of chess. The Roman army was outmaneuvered, outguessed, outfought, completely defeated. That night forty-four thousand Romans lay dead on the battlefield; the bodies included those of ex-consuls, generals, senators, most of the aristocracy of Rome; and a bushel of gold rings was taken from the fingers of Roman knights and sent to Carthage.

But Hannibal lost the war through the inertia of his countrymen. While he waited for reinforcements Rome raised new armies, recovered her revolted provinces, seized Spain, and moved on Carthage herself. Too late, Hannibal's brother Hasdrubal set out with Spanish troops; they were destroyed in central Italy, and Hasdrubal's severed head was thrown into Hannibal's camp. A belated fleet from Carthage was blown out of its course and caught by Roman ships off Sardinia. Finally Hannibal was hastily recalled to Africa to raise a defensive army. His military genius was of no avail. At Zama, in 202 B. C., Hannibal's raw mercenaries were cut to pieces by the disciplined legions of young Scipio Africanus. Again Carthage sued for peace.

This Second Punic War was the end of Carthaginian power. Carthage became a vassal of Rome, forbidden to make war save with Roman permission. She had to pay the Romans two hundred talents every year for fifty years. And her mighty fleet was disbanded—all but ten triremes.

Rome now ruled supreme in the west, and was ready to bring a fresh ascendancy to Hellenistic culture. Her great coin, the denarius—based on the Attic standard—replaced the "Phoenician standard" of Carthage. Rome herself had long ago come under the influence of Magna Graecia, as the Greek cities of Sicily were called. And the most famous of these cities, Syracuse, had become hers during the Second Punic War.

That rich and cultured Sicilian capital, filled with the finest Hellenic art, had enjoyed peace and prosperity for fifty-four years under Hieron II. During his remarkable reign no honest citizen was killed, exiled, or injured. And Archimedes, the greatest inventor of the ancient world, lived and worked in Syracuse under this beneficent rule. Unfortunately, Hieron's successor, Hieronymus, broke the treaty of alliance with Rome and invited in the Carthaginians. So in 212 B. C. the Romans sent an army under the Consul Marcellus to attack Syracuse.

The city's brave defense was aided by the science of Archimedes. His immense catapults hurled great stones into the midst of the advancing legions; his cranes along the city's sea-walls dropped heavy weights that sank ships venturing too near. But finally, after eight months of siege, the starved Syracusans surrendered—and the greatest Greek metropolis of the west fell to Rome.

Now that Carthage had been humbled, Rome struck eastward to take over the rest of the collapsing Greek world. At Cynoscephalae ("Dogs' Heads"), in 197 B. C., her legions crushed Philip V of Macedon, who had rashly made an alliance with Hannibal. Philip was allowed to keep his throne but not his Greek possessions. "All Greece," the Consul Flaminius declared at the Isthmian Games, "is to be free!" But in just seven years the Greeks were begging the Seleucid Emperor, Antiochus III, to free them from this "Roman peace." Rome welcomed the challenge: her troops under the Scipio brothers ("Africanus" and "Asiaticus") smashed the allied army at Magnesia in Asia Minor; the Aetolian League was dissolved, and all the land west of the Halys River went to Rome's ally Pergamum, which was to be a future province. Seventeen years later, Rome defeated a new eastern coalition—of

Macedonia under Philip's son Perseus, Seleucus IV, and the island of
Rhodes. Now she took over Ionia and Macedon and ordered dissolution
of Corinth's Achaean League, which had encouraged Perseus. For
answer, angry Corinthian women emptied slops on the heads of a
senatorial delegation! Punishment was swift and terrible: the legions
of Consul Mommius overpowered Corinth; the city was razed, its
men killed, its women enslaved. This was the end of Greece as a free
nation.

So Hellas at last fell to Rome, but only militarily. Soon a new
slogan was current: "Captive Greece has taken her conqueror captive!"
For the Hellenization of Rome now reached a flood-tide as a result of
all these conquests. From the spoils of Syracuse to the sack of Corinth,
captured Greek treasures poured into Rome; countless libraries, statues, paintings. Roman generals, senators, and tax-farmers built themselves sumptuous Greek-style palaces; and Rome erected new public
buildings, basilicas, colonnades, theaters, all in the Hellenistic manner.
Cultured Greeks, hostages and captives and slaves, swarmed through
the city of Rome—"The City," it was called—teaching and lecturing,
serving as scribes and secretaries, spreading Hellenic learning, philosophy, and science. Thousands of Romans spoke and wrote Greek, and
the well-to-do sent their sons to Greece to "finish" their education.
And Greek literature burst upon the Romans in translations and adap-
tations and imitations that profoundly changed their own stiff language.
A freed Greek slave put the *Odyssey* into Latin verse; Ennius initiated
Roman poetry with his patriotic *Annals* in a meter borrowed from the
Greek; and Plautus and Terence wrote popular and elegant Roman
comedies, freely inspired by the Greek plays of Menander, master of
the Attic "new comedy." So overwhelming was the Hellenistic vogue
that it was attacked by the arch-conservatives led by the Censor Cato.
Significantly, the rival phil-Hellenic (or pro-Greek) circle was headed
by none other than Scipio Africanus.

For Rome, now Hellenized, was moving irresistibly toward her
destiny. Egypt was already her protectorate under a friendship treaty.

SLAVE MART—ROME

In this Roman slave market a Semitic trader is selling slaves. On the block stands a young Greek. If he has been educated, he will bring a high price. With good fortune, he may then become his master's friend and the teacher of his master's children; and in time he may be given his freedom. Otherwise, with his powerful body, he may end his days in a mine or an arena. Slaves were displayed naked so prospective buyers could examine them for physical defects or disease, as they might a horse.

Corinth fell to her in 146 B. C.; and the same year saw the terrible destruction of Carthage, carried out by Scipio himself. His army arrived in Africa with harsh new demands and an order that Carthaginians abandon their port and settle inland. Carthage heroically refused; a quarter of a million men, women, and children died in the siege and the final massacre, and fifty thousand survivors were sold into slavery. The great city was leveled, "blotted out" as Cato had urged, its site cursed and sown with salt. Now there was no nation left in the Mediterranean world strong enough to oppose the might of a triumphant Rome.

ROMAN STREET SCENE

It is the year 52 B. C., and Rome is now the great city of the world! In these pictures you see senators, legionaries, citizens, slaves, and subjects from the Asiatic provinces and Greece and Egypt—all of them waiting to see and cheer the triumph of Caesar and his victorious legions, just returned from the Gallic Wars. Visitors are still streaming into the already crowded city, increasing the confusion. They have come to see a show, to see the hero of the hour, to see mighty Caesar.

X.   Imperial Rome

146 B. C. - A. D. 14

In the next century and a half the circle of Roman power around the Mediterranean was completed. And the circle of Mediterranean civilization was completed too.

For the first time one all-inclusive empire was created along the shores of what the Romans called *Mare Nostrum*—"Our Sea." Spain, Gaul, Italy, Greece, Palestine, Mesopotamia, Egypt, North Africa, the

The procession passes. First comes Caesar himself in a toga of Tyrian purple, driving a golden chariot drawn by four horses. Next are his captains. Behind them walk the Gallic prisoners in chains, headed by Vercingetorix, the betrayed chieftain, and jeered at by the Roman crowd on their path to death. The legions follow, each soldier with a captive slave given him by the conqueror. A long line of wagons laden with loot ends the triumphal march. The next few days will be gloriously filled with gladiatorial games financed by Caesar.

whole vast perimeter came under a single government. Every surrounding land, from the oldest and most civilized to the youngest and most barbarian, was thrown at last into the great melting-pot of imperial Rome.

The birth of this empire was a painful process. Those same invincible legions that had brutally subjugated countries abroad now engaged in terrible convulsions at home. The Roman Republic, the second great ancient attempt at self-government, collapsed in an orgy of civil wars even bloodier than those that had destroyed democratic Greece. Yet, for all the bloodshed that brought it into being, the new Roman Empire achieved much for Western man.

For the Romans had talents that set them above all ancient conquerors from Sargon to Alexander. Like others before them, these rude and sturdy soldier-farmers had learned civilization from the superior nations they had overcome: the Etruscans, the Carthaginians, the Greeks. But from the beginning, the Romans *gave* something unique. In all their conquests, starting with the Latin League, diplomacy played as vital a part as the "invincible legions." Alliances were not only for making war. The vanquished too were offered treaties; they were made partners, so to speak, in the growing Roman community. Here was Alexander's fevered dream of *homonoia,* or concord, brought down to earth and put to a practical use. And these forthright Romans showed the same common sense in administering their vast empire.

Under Rome's organizing genius the Mediterranean area was finally fused into one cultural world. Rome preserved and developed the gifts of many peoples, though often destroying the nations that produced them. Her roads and sea-lanes quickened communications and commerce between the most distant territories. Her vast public works—aqueducts, baths, amphitheaters—were unrivaled till modern times. Politically, she made gigantic strides, extending the privileges of Roman citizenship and the protection of Roman law to every free man in the Empire. Above all, Rome consolidated the advances of thousands of years into one final flowering of ancient civilization.

TRAMPING LEGIONS: THE REPUBLIC DIES, THE EMPIRE IS BORN

The Roman Empire was born in an ordeal of bloodshed: even as her legions completed the march of conquest abroad, at home they swept her into cataclysmic civil wars.

In two centuries, the Republic had risen from Italian state to Mediterranean power, but all the while the domestic situation grew more dangerous. Too often the peasant-soldier returning from the wars found only poverty: his house in ruins, his fields destroyed, his family scattered. Unable to compete with slave labor on the estates of the wealthy, he sold his land for a pittance and joined the landless masses in Rome. But the government did nothing. Even public lands, instead of being distributed, were seized by the avaricious rich. The fatal gulf between the Senate and the people, between the haves and the have-nots, grew ever wider.

A few courageous nobles tried in vain to stem the tide of injustices. Most noted of the patrician liberals were the Gracchi, Tiberius and his brother Gaius. Elected a tribune by the Assembly in 133 B. C., Tiberius introduced a land-reform law with these famous words: "The beasts of the field and the birds of the air have their holes and their hiding places; but men who fight and die for Italy enjoy only the light and the air. . . . You are called the masters of the world, but there is not a foot of ground that you can call your own." But a vindictive Senate accused him of harboring dictatorial ambitions and had him impeached. Then a riot was started in the Forum, where the vote was to be taken. Tiberius and his retainers were killed, and his body thrown in the Tiber. Undismayed, Gaius continued the task, becoming a tribune himself in 124 B. C., and obtaining passage of a number of radical laws. But while he was absent in Africa his foes changed the voting set-up so that he was defeated for re-election on his return; and a year later the Senate moved to repeal the Gracchan laws. Another riot followed, three thousand of Gaius's party were killed by senatorial decree, and his corpse followed his brother's into the Tiber.

Worse violence was to come. For now Rome fell under the sway of military commanders, who began to exploit this class conflict in open warfare. For a century Roman army fought Roman army, to the accompaniment of assassinations and mob violence, with patrician and plebeian heads displayed on pikes.

The first soldier-statesman was Marius, idol of the popular party. He was chosen consul in 107 B. C., was re-elected six times, and won fame for his victories abroad—first over Jugurtha, King of Numidia in North Africa, then over the Celtic hordes that were threatening Rome. At his second triumph, Marius was named "savior of the Republic." But he had set a dangerous precedent: he was the victor, the hero, the demagogue. And he reorganized the Roman legions into a well-paid professional force, ready to do the bidding of their commander even against Rome itself.

The danger became real under the patrician leader Sulla. Acclaimed for putting down the Social War—an insurrection of Italian cities seeking agrarian reform and political equality—this new hero easily won election as consul. But when the Senate named him to command the eastern army Sulla marched on the capital and installed a reactionary regime with repressive laws. Then he left for the east, and the civil war began again. The aged Marius entered Rome with a new army, the streets ran with the blood of massacred patricians, and the radicals ruled briefly. But Sulla cut short his victorious campaign against King Mithradates in Asia Minor and hurried back. In Rome he defeated an army led by the son of Marius, won a savage contest with the forces of the assembly, had himself proclaimed Dictator, and cruelly re-established aristocratic rule. Now Rome knew the horror of "proscription": lists of prominent men were posted daily in the Forum, their lives and property forfeit, as enemies of the state.

During these fratricidal wars, slave uprisings were constant throughout the country, for not only Rome but all of Italy was teeming with slaves. They came from every captured province; there were Gauls, Spaniards, Africans, Egyptians, Illyrians, Macedonians, Thracians, Syrians, and Greeks. From time to time these doomed captives staged brief, futile escapes. But in 73 B. C. the Revolt of the Gladiators reached terrifying proportions. Originally seventy-eight slaves broke out of a gladiatorial school at Capua and fled to the slopes of Vesuvius, where they chose a Thracian named Spartacus for their captain. Other slaves streamed to join them, till Spartacus had a force of seventy thousand, armed with stolen or homemade weapons. His army won victory after victory over the regulars, and its numbers swelled to one hundred and twenty thousand, but the slaves could not fulfill their objective of escaping from Italy. Finally cornered at Thurii in the south, many deserted to the enemy, but Spartacus and a loyal band

died on the field of battle. Six thousand wretched survivors were cruci-
fied along the Appian Way.

In such turbulent times, the Romans continued to choose soldiers
as consuls. And soon the old rivalry of Marius and Sulla was being re-
enacted on a climactic scale by two new generals and demagogues:
Julius Caesar, leader of the popular party and conqueror of the European West; and Pompey, the aristocratic leader and conqueror of the
Asiatic East.

Pompey gained renown by a swift campaign that freed the Mediterranean and adjoining seas of pirates. Then, commanding the army
of the east, he won a series of brilliant victories: Mithradates finally
surrendered, and Armenia, Syria, and Judea became Roman provinces.
In 62 B. C. Pompey returned home, loaded with plunder, to enjoy a
hero's triumph.

But in Rome he encountered Caesar—a nephew of Marius, and
the ambitious new head of the *populares*. Pompey needed Caesar's help
to secure approval of the eastern treaties. So a strange political alliance
was born, the Triumvirate: Pompey, Caesar, and the wealthy Crassus.
By this plan, Caesar was elected Consul; in 59 B. C. he pushed his agrarian reform-laws through the Senate, and at forty-one he became commander of the army of the west and governor of Illyria and Gaul.
Within eight years Caesar's legions had reached the English channel,
all Gaul had been subdued, and the Germans were held at the Rhine.
And the popular politician-general publicized his own victories by
writing an account of the Gallic Wars.

Conflict between the two rivals was now certain, for the third
triumvir had died fighting the savage Parthians. Pompey struck first:
in Rome he switched back to the senatorial party and agreed to command its army, and the Senate ordered Caesar to disband his legions.
Then Caesar made his historic decision: he crossed the Rubicon River
into Italy and marched on Rome!

Pompey fled to Greece and started to assemble a large army; and
groups of frightened senators, and rich men and their ladies went

with him. But Caesar was moving with lightning speed: in Rome he was re-elected Consul immediately; next he cut off the senatorial troops in Spain and received their surrender; then he embarked for Greece and routed Pompey's army in Thessaly. Pompey himself escaped to Egypt in a small boat but was assassinated as he stepped ashore. Victorious Caesar followed and was greeted with open arms by Cleopatra, last of the Ptolemaic line. This beautiful queen tried all her charms on the conqueror, but after nine months of dalliance Caesar bade her farewell and returned to war. He suppressed revolts in Asia, won victories in North Africa and Spain, and returned to Rome as master of the Empire.

Now, for a few short years, Caesar displayed statesmanship. He was given the title of Dictator for life, but he took no personal revenge; there were no massacres or proscriptions as in the days of Marius and Sulla. Though he was deified and ruled as a despot, the political form of the Republic remained unchanged. If anything, it was democratized. For Caesar sought to limit the power of the aristocratic Senate by increasing its membership to include representatives of new Roman families. And he introduced sweeping reforms, reorganizing the administration of justice, appointing upright provincial governors, stopping corruption in government offices. In addition, he decreed the revision of the calendar, started a huge project of rebuilding Rome, and laid out vast public works for the rest of Italy; he even planned to drain the Pontine marshes. But the jealous Senate resented everything he suggested, especially his laws extending Roman citizenship to provincials and granting self-rule to Italian towns.

On the "Ides of March," March 15, 44 B. C., a spring day with a blue sky, a day of rumors and portents and evil omens, this resentment burst into murder in the Senate theater. At the age of fifty-six, Julius Caesar, politician, soldier, statesman, was stabbed to death by twenty-three envious and fanatical senators before the statue of his enemy, Pompey the Great.

This reckless assassination loosed the final storm—Rome was swept into one last awful convulsion of civil war.

THE DEATH OF CAESAR

Here, before the statue of Pompey, Caesar was stabbed. Cassius struck first; the others followed. When Brutus struck, Caesar, drawing his robe across his face, fell and died at the foot of the statue of his great antagonist. So perished the greatest of Romans!

It started with the dread days of the Second Triumvirate. As heir Caesar had left his grand-nephew and adopted son Octavian, a frail and sickly boy of eighteen whom the politicians ignored. But the youth soon won army support, victories, and election to the consulate. Then, in imitation of his famous uncle, he formed a coalition of rivals: Octavian, Antony, and the Consul Lepidus. The three needed money, and they proceeded to collect it by proscription in the worst reign of terror in Roman history. List after list was posted; three hundred senators and two thousand members of the Equestrian Order were put to death and their estates confiscated. Slaves were paid as much as ten thousand drachmas for murdering their convicted masters. Among the great men proscribed was the famous orator Cicero, who tried in vain to escape by sea; his head and right hand were hung on a Forum wall!

Overseas there was more bloodshed, as the new triumvirs eliminated Caesar's assassins and then turned on each other. Brutus and Cassius fled to Greece and seized command of the Army of the east; Octavian and Antony pursued with their legions, and defeated the last senatorial army at Philippi in Macedonia. (The conspirators fell on their own swords.) Now the Triumvirate divided up Rome's vast territories: the east to Antony, the west to Octavian, and Africa to Lepidus. But Lepidus attempted to seize Sicily and was deposed. Then Antony married the power-hungry Cleopatra and presented Rome's eastern possessions to her. And now Octavian moved. Off the Greek coast, at Actium, his fleet defeated the warships of Antony and Cleopatra. The ambitious pair fled to Alexandria, where they committed suicide; Antony stabbed himself, and Cleopatra allowed herself to be bitten by an asp.

At last, Octavian ruled supreme over the whole vast empire. When he returned to Rome an obsequious Senate hastily conferred upon him the designation of "Augustus"; soon afterward he was made *Principes* or first citizen, and *Imperator* or commander-in-chief. With all these titles, and with the support of his faithful legions, Octavian became in name and in fact the first Emperor of Rome.

THE AUGUSTAN AGE

As the Emperor Augustus, Octavian was to rule forty-four years with a statesman's vision and justice. Gone was the merciless youth who had risen to power through a series of melodramatic horrors. Gone too were

AUGUSTUS

Octavian Augustus, first Emperor of Rome, is shown here, full-armored and with a retinue of subservient senators—the very figure of greatness. This portrait is drawn after a flattering contemporary statue now in the Vatican. The unknown sculptor showed Augustus as physically overpowering, when as a matter of fact the emperor was of average build and was plagued all his life by many ills. As a youth, with Mark Antony and Lepidus, he started a reign of terror more bloody than Rome had ever before suffered. But on gaining absolute power, he became a just, honest, patient, and merciful ruler. Although his power grew from day to day, he never abused it. By no means a great military leader, he was an amazing statesman, which was what Rome needed. He controlled the senate, Rome, and the provinces; rebuilt the city, restoring her temples and erecting new ones; and supported literature and the arts.

the turmoil and devastation of a hundred years of civil war. Rome and her provinces needed peace and order and rebuilding; they got all that, and much more, in the golden years of the Augustan Age.

Augustus's first task was to send his legions to the frontiers of the empire. He rebuilt fortifications; he constructed new military roads and repaired old ones. This done, he turned to a thorough reorganization of the civil government: he reformed the bureaucracy, and appointed honest provincial governors who were responsible directly to him. Conquered lands had suffered particularly from infamous extortion and the usury of moneylenders. But now Augustus put an end to these corrupt practices and introduced a virtual government monopoly of the banking business. Under his reforms the whole empire entered a new era of thriving commerce.

And Rome, the imperial city herself, was completely renovated. After the ravages of a century of riots and street-fighting and neglect, there were a thousand things to be done. Augustus, a great organizer, saw to all of them. With the immense wealth of the empire he rebuilt Rome more magnificently than Caesar had dreamed. He constructed great aqueducts, baths, temples, theaters, libraries, forums; and he used to boast proudly, "I found Rome a city of brick and made it a city of marble."

In this rebuilding the Romans showed their tremendous skill at architecture and engineering. Of course Rome's architects had borrowed columns and ornamental developments (like the Alexandrian portico) from the Greeks, but they went far beyond their models. In a sense, Hellenic architecture was imprisoned by its own beauty. The Greek temple achieved perfection, but it evolved from a basic plan that hardly changed. When Pericles was rebuilding the Acropolis, that high cliff called for a monumental total design; yet his architects clung to their orthodox temple-plan, and each building was set on a different axis and had no relation in size to the others. The Romans, on the contrary, were the boldest innovators. Improving on the Etruscan arch and vault, and introducing the use of concrete, they produced a new Roman style in a truly grand manner: imposing bridges and triumphal arches, structures with lofty unencumbered domes, aqueducts stretching hundreds of miles on arched supports to bring water into the capital.

The Emperor's new city was full of sculpture too, though in this art the Romans usually imitated the Greeks. It was a matter of fashion as much as of aesthetics. Little original work was done by Roman sculptors, since most of their time went in copying the pillaged Grecian masterpieces that were in such great demand. Only in one type of sculpture did the Romans excel: their lifelike portraits have never been equaled except in the Renaissance. And they perfected the pictorial bas-relief that would embellish countless triumphal arches—it was used on Augustus' Altar of Peace, the showpiece of his metropolis.

For Augustan Rome was really a "big city," the largest in Europe. Now it had splendid sights: the new Forum of travertine and tufa, all paved in marble, the new park on the Field of Mars, with Augustus' mausoleum and groves of evergreens and Greek and Latin libraries. And the Emperor even sought to relieve congestion in the slums: he limited the height of flimsy wooden tenements to four stories, and organized a protective fire brigade. The population was nearing the million mark, and the streets were crowded not only with Roman citizens who wore the toga, but with Syrians, Egyptians, Greeks, Gauls, Spaniards, Africans, slaves and settlers, who gave the city a cosmopolitan tone. Rome was now visibly the capital of the civilized world.

Yet the most enduring achievement of the Augustan Age was not its monuments but its literature. Here, too, Greek influence remained strong. But writers now displayed great original genius, and they owed much to two famous sponsors: the wealthy Maecenas, whose name has become a synonym for "patron of the arts," and the Emperor himself. To be sure, Roman literature had its foundation in the period just preceding. Cicero, the famous Republican statesman and "Father of His Country," had created a rich Latin prose in his majestic and sonorous orations. Lucretius had composed a vast philosophical poem *On the Nature of the Universe*, and shaped fresh words from the "poverty" of his native tongue. And Catullus had written passionate love lyrics, in exquisite Greek-style meters.

But now came the Golden Age of Roman poetry. Under Augustus, Horace composed his famous Odes, which still seem to breathe the fresh country air. And the literary world was dominated by Virgil, greatest of all Roman poets. Already famous at thirty-two for his *Georgics* on the joys of rural life, he was commissioned by the Emperor to write an epic about the founding of Rome. For ten years Virgil labored on his masterpiece—the tale of burning Troy, of heroic Aeneas, of Venus and Mars. Then he died, begging his friends to destroy the still unfinished poem. But Augustus wisely forbade it and the *Aeneid*, singing triumphantly of Roman glory, lives today as one of the immortal epics of mankind.

Yet it was a prose writer who came closest to expressing the ideals of Augustus himself. Livy spent forty years writing his great chronicle of Roman history; it occupied one hundred and forty-two books, though only thirty-five remain. An ultra-conservative, a believer in the stern virtues of old Rome and all her sacred rites, he echoed the views of his ruler, in whom he found a true friend.

For Augustus, during all his reign, sought to revive the ancient virtues and the ancient faith. Not that earlier citizens had been religious. Their tribal gods, like the Etruscans', paralleled the half-human Greek divinities, though the Romans did envision them as spirits of field and lake and hill who guarded human beings from birth to death. But the old rituals were strongly patriotic; great numbers of clergy, supported and controlled by the state, served the temples and conducted festivals under an elected Chief Priest or Pontifex Maximus. And these old-time ceremonies Augustus restored. In his latter years, however, the Emperor turned strict moralist, even going so far as to banish the poet Ovid, author of the witty but improper *Metamorphoses,* and to have his own granddaughter tried and exiled for immorality. Yet despite the pious excesses of his old age and the brutality of his youth, Augustus was a great ruler. When he died (in A. D. 14) at the age of seventy-six—he was cremated on the Field of Mars and made a god— all Rome mourned the passing of the splendid Augustan Age.

THE HERITAGE

With the death of Augustus, our narrative of the first three thousand years of Mediterranean civilization comes to a close. But the story really has no end.

The Roman Empire was to last another five centuries, through good and bad emperors, from the philosopher Marcus Aurelius to Nero the matricide. The period was marked by violence, invasions, plagues, assassinations, civil wars, and wars of conquest. Yet for many generations Rome kept her highways and sea-lanes safe for world travel and commerce. A uniform system of law was enforced, even to the Empire's farthest frontiers. In Asia, Europe, and Africa, the Romans built stupendous temples, theaters, baths, aqueducts, and roads—and built them so well that many still stand today. By Trajan's time, after the end of the first century, Rome was incomparably the greatest city in the known world; eleven emperors after Augustus had adorned her lavishly with Greek art and monumental architecture. All told, the Empire gave men four hundred years of relative stability, the Pax Romana or "Roman peace"; and for another century Rome fought back the barbarian hordes.

Finally the Roman Empire broke into two parts, and the barbarians pressed in upon it—Saxons, Franks, Vandals, Alamanni, Goths, Ostrogoths, Visigoths, and Attila's Huns. But when Rome collapsed she left much to the Western world: her laws and ordered government, her concept of justice, her realistic and direct approach to life, her vast public works. Some of these gifts she passed on directly; Latin was the universal language of Europe in the Middle Ages. Other gifts were, in a sense, deferred and forgotten till the great cultural revival of the Renaissance. But all of Rome's culture became part of the Western heritage, and all of it was founded upon past millennia.

Livy, the historian, had written of Rome with fervent patriotism. He was well aware that though the Republic might be dead, the Empire

ROME NEARS HER END

These two pictures show the destruction of a small Roman city by
an invading tribe. Similar scenes, hardly differing in detail, marked
the collapse of the entire Empire. On all sides Rome was surrounded
by barbarians—Visigoths, Ostrogoths, Gauls, Saxons, Franks, Vandals,
Huns, Scythians—who marched and counter-marched from town
to town, spreading death by fire and sword. It was the barbarians'
answer to their suffering of centuries under Roman brutality. After
these successful raids they settled down and took over the provinces
of Rome.

was established upon its foundations—on the Republic's conquests,
laws, and military discipline. What Livy did not realize was that Rome
was also built on all the cultures that had preceded her around the
Mediterranean. She owed a debt not only to the lands she imitated,
such as Greece, but also to countries that had already decayed and

But the barbarian leaders soon ruled as kings and fought one another. Thus in A. D. 400 the Visigoths crossed the Alps into Italy, and ten years later captured Rome. Meanwhile the Vandals crossed the Rhine in A. D. 408, ravaged France and Spain, reached Africa by the Strait of Gibraltar, and captured Carthage in A. D. 429. Sixteen years later they sailed across the Mediterranean and landed at the Tiber's mouth, marching inland to drive out the Visigoths and become the new masters of Rome. Such was the strange, mixed-up world in which the Roman Empire disintegrated!

fallen. It was in Hammurabi's Babylon that law was first codified, and the Persian Empire built the first great highway system. And these past civilizations did not die; they only seemed to.

Today, for instance, all along the Nile we can see the remains of

Egypt's might—colossal ruins of diorite, granite, and limestone, broken by earthquake and time. Great lonely columns are reflected in the rivers and abandoned figures of gods and kings face the morning sun. Pyramids, obelisks, and temples rise desolate against the blue sky; and in the western hills empty tombs, carved in living rock, vainly await the return of their long-lost Pharaohs. But is ancient Egypt really dead? The Egyptians were the earliest to devise a calendar. And it was to Egypt, to the Alexandrian astronomer Sosigenes that Caesar turned when he reformed the Roman calendar, to produce a system of months and days, which—with some later corrections—we still use.

Thus it was with much of the culture of imperial Rome. Her alphabet—our own alphabet—came from the letters the Phoenician traders had taught the barbarian Greeks. Her great arches and vaults derived from the earliest civilization of the Near East, ancient Sumer. And Babylonian and Sumerian was her division of time by the sexagesimal system into a day of two twelve-hour periods, with sixty minutes to the hour, and sixty seconds to the minute—as on all our clocks. Indeed, the typical Roman aqueducts were but the latest development of water-control, which Western man first contrived in the valley of the Nile and the valley of the River of Paradise. For countless nations, large and small, had poured their gifts into one great, slow stream of history that had flowed clear around the Mediterranean. And when the mighty Roman Empire took over the area she inherited it all—a Babel of many countries and peoples, with a conglomeration of ancient cultures and a multitude of strange and sometimes foul gods.

Yet the light of idealism was embedded in the Empire too, no matter how harshly it was obscured. In A. D. 70, after two centuries of oppression and rebellion, the Emperor Titus finally razed the city of Jerusalem and the temple. Yet the "People of the Book" survived, and their ethics and aspirations lived on in the pages of the Old Testament. And during the reign of Augustus, in the Palestinian village of Bethlehem, was born a Child whose followers would spread the message of the New Testament throughout the Roman Empire, despite cruel persecution—till Rome herself fell, and the West bore the name of Christendom.

But Rome did not really die, either. True, her world-empire finally rotted away under the cancer of slavery and economic and moral collapse. And in A. D. 476 Romulus Augustulus (named for her founder and first emperor) was deposed by an army of German mercenaries who made their leader, Odoacer, king of Italy. But he promptly acknowledged himself a vassal of the eastern Roman Empire. That Eastern Empire lasted nearly a thousand years in Constantinople, until it was captured by the Ottoman Turks in A. D. 1453. In the West, a millennium after the fall of Rome, came the Renaissance or "rebirth" of ancient civilization. It spread to all fields, art, literature, science, even navigation: in A. D. 1492 Columbus discovered America! Thus the stream of history flowed on, through Europe and the New World.

So it was not only the culture of imperial Rome, but all Western civilization that had its thrilling beginnings in the Mediterranean area —in the splendor and brutality, the beauty and wisdom, the tools and science and art, and the lasting spiritual values of the first three thousand years.

Reading List

GENERAL

Casson, Lionel. *The Ancient Mariners.* (New York: Macmillan, 1959.) Trade, piracy, sea fights, and all the romance and dangers of the deep.

Ceram, C. W. *Gods, Graves, and Scholars: The Story of Archaeology.* (New York: Knopf, 1951.) How the fabled treasures of Troy, Crete, Egypt, Assyria, Sumer, etc., were restored to mankind.

Lissner, Ivar. *The Living Past.* (New York: Putnam, 1957.) Brief, brilliant sketches of early civilizations.

SPECIFIC

Egypt

Mayer, Josephine, and Prideaux, Tom. *Never to Die: The Egyptians in Their Own Words.* (New York: Viking, 1938.) Egyptian stories, poems, letters, sayings, beautifully illustrated with ancient drawings and sculptures.

Wilson, John Albert. *The Culture of Ancient Egypt.* (Chicago: University of Chicago, Phoenix [paper], 1956.)

Mesopotamia

Chiera, Edward. *They Wrote on Clay: The Babylonian Tablets Speak Today.* (Chicago: University of Chicago, 1938; Phoenix [paper], 1955.) The exciting world of the cuneiform tablets.

Contenau, Georges. *Everyday Life in Babylon and Assyria.* (New York: St. Martin's Press, 1954.) In a breezy style, a noted scholar covers everything imaginable from soap to armies to dream.

Kramer, Samuel Noah. *History Begins at Sumer.* (New York: Doubleday, Anchor [paper], 1959.) Twenty-five Sumerian "firsts," from the first case of apple-polishing to the first love song.

Asia Minor and Palestine

Gaster, Theodor H. *The Oldest Stories in the World.* (New York: Viking, 1952; Boston: Beacon [paper], 1959.) Babylonian, Hittite, and Canaanite legends in original translations, starting with the famous adventures of Gilgamesh.

Keller, Werner. *The Bible as History: A Confirmation of the Book of Books.* (New York: Morrow, 1956.) A thrilling account of the latest archaeological finds and the way they bear out the beloved Bible stories.

Greece and the Hellenic World

Bonnard, André. *Greek Civilization:* Volume I, *From the Iliad to the Parthenon.* (New York: Macmillan, 1957.) Volume II, *From the Antigone to Socrates.* (New York: Macmillan, 1959.) Glowing chapters recreate the ancient culture to which we probably owe the most.

Robinson, C. E. *Hellas: A Short History of Ancient Greece.* (New York: Pantheon, 1948; Boston: Beacon [paper], 1955.) An engrossing piece of story-telling, with line drawings by the author.

Etruria and Rome

Bloch, Raymond. *The Etruscans.* (New York: Praeger, 1958.) All that we know about these mysterious people.

Gross-Hodge, Humphrey. *Roman Panorama: A Background for Today.* (Cambridge, England: Cambridge University, 1944.) A lively conducted tour of Rome and her empire.

Radin, Max. *Epicurus, My Master.* (Chapel Hill: University of North Carolina, 1949.) In the last days of the Roman Republic, Pomponius Atticus reflects on "country life and civic strife" and famous men he has known.

Waddy, Lawrence. *Pax Romana and World Peace.* (New York: Norton, 1951.) A lively and penetrating study of the achievements and failures of the Roman Empire — and their bearing on peace for the modern world.

Index

Pronunciation Key: ā āte; ă ăt; ȧ senȧte; ä ärm; ȧ ȧsk; â câre; ĕ mĕt; ē bē; ê ênough; ẽ hẽr; ĭ ĭt; ī īce; ŏ nŏt; ō nōte; ȯ ȯbey; ô hôrse; ŭ ŭs; ū ūse; û ûnite; û fûr; ŏŏ fŏŏt; ōō fōōd.